This Book Belongs To:

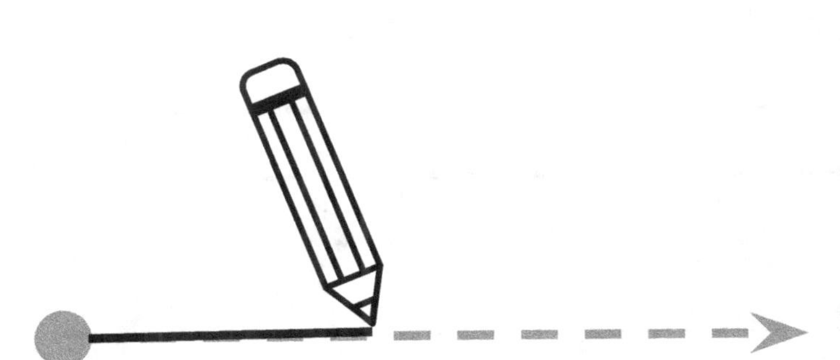

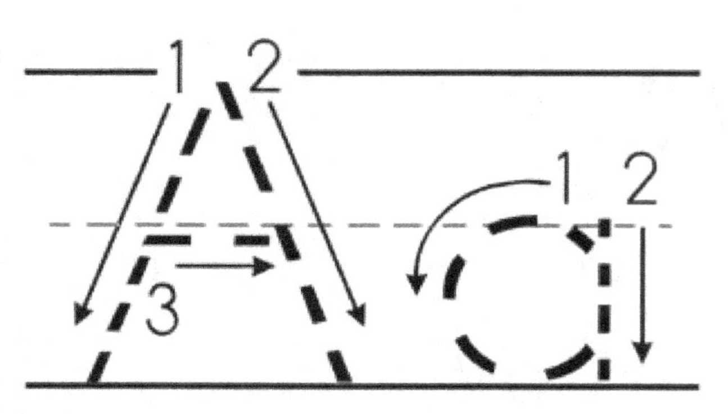

TRACE THE LETTERS AND WRITE YOUR OWN ON THE REMAINING LINE

A A A A A A A

A A A A A A A

A A A A A A A

A A A A A A A

A A A A A A A

A A A A A A A

a a a a a a a

a a a a a a a

a a a a a a a

a a a a a a a

a a a a a a a

Trace the letters and write your own on the remaining line.

B B B B B B B

B B B B B B B

B B B B B B B

B B B B B B B

B B B B B B B

B B B B B B B

Trace the letters and write your own on the remaining line.

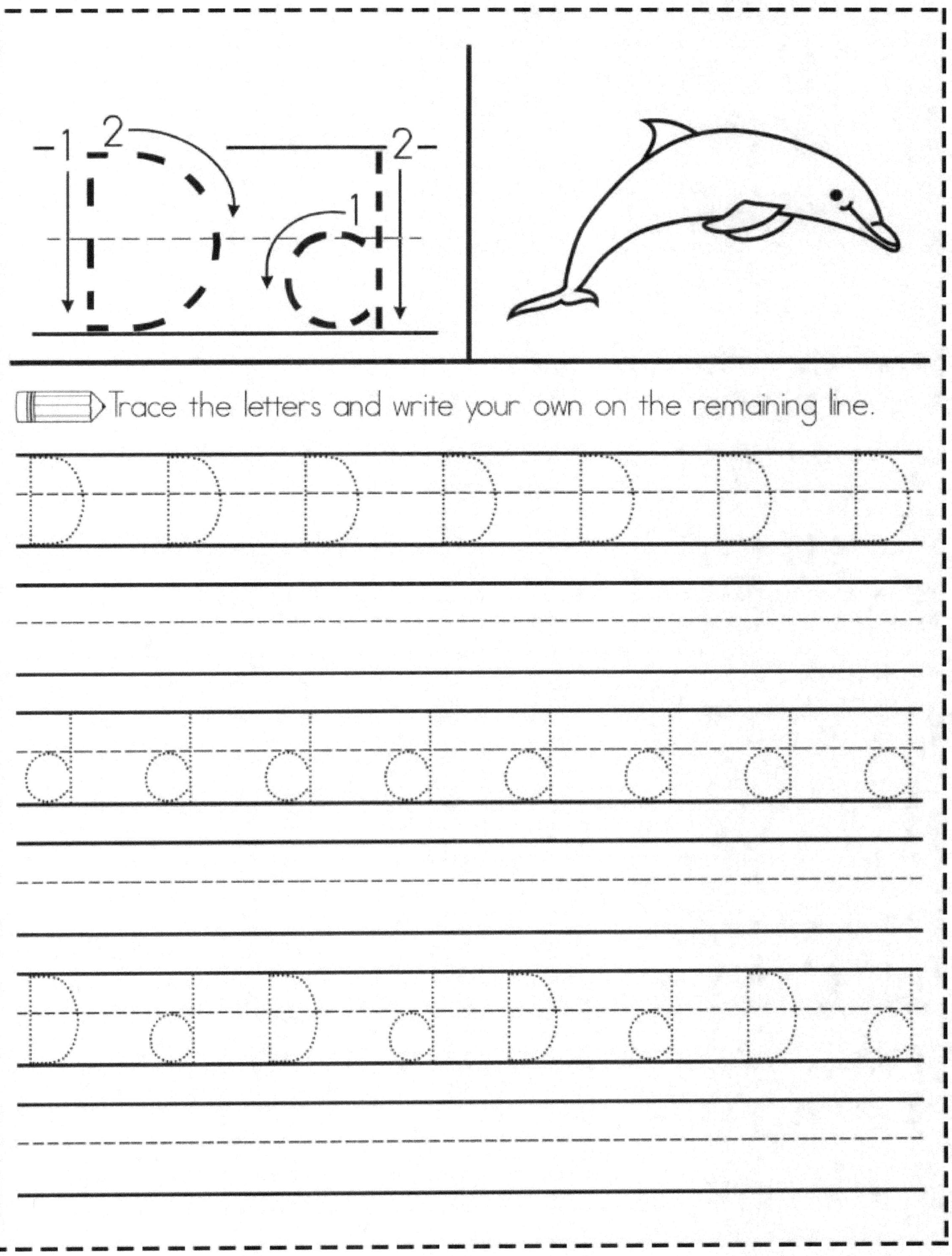

-1 2
2-
1
Trace the letters and write your own on the remaining line.

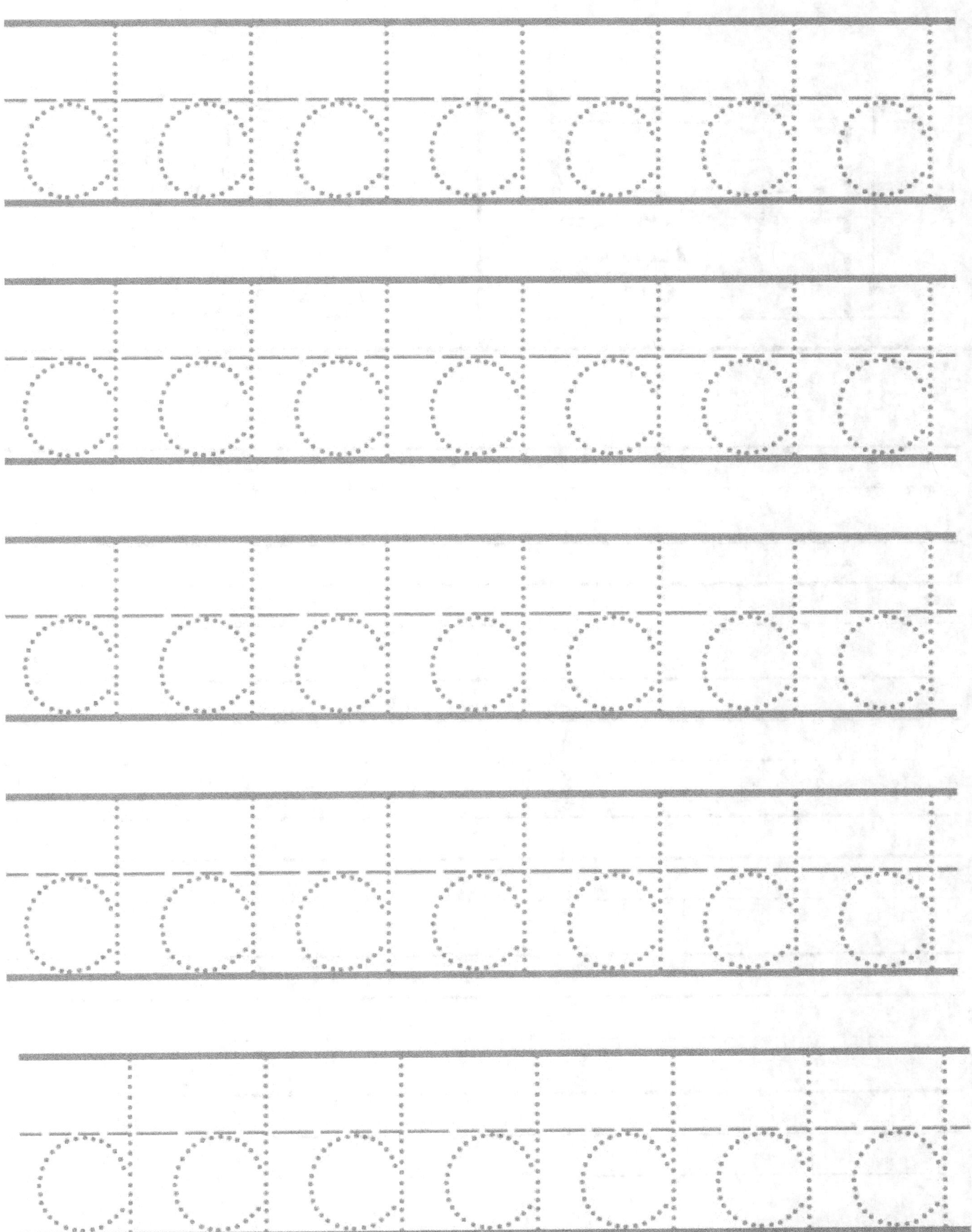

Trace the letters and write your own on the remaining line.

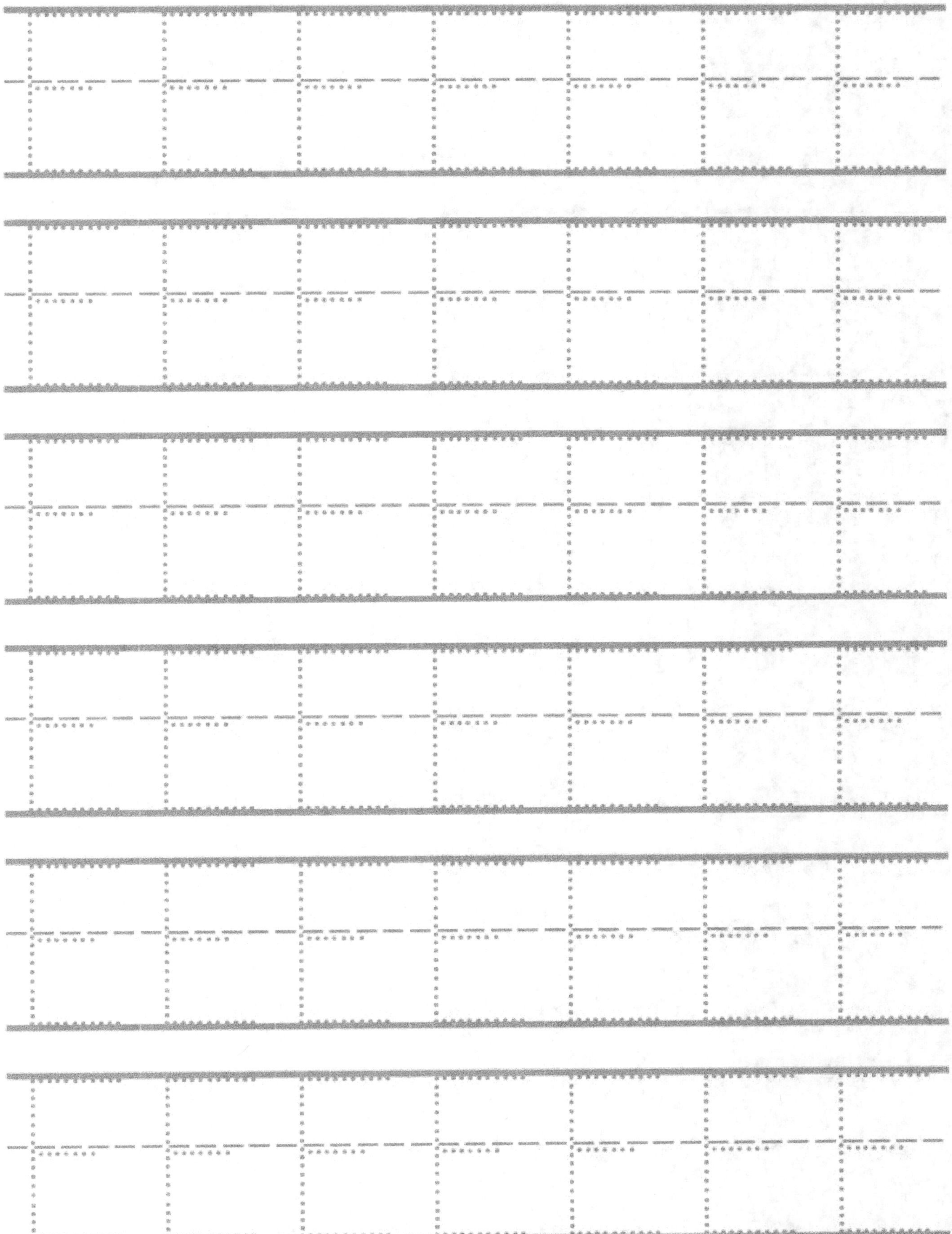

e e e e e e e

e e e e e e e

e e e e e e e

e e e e e e e

e e e e e e e

e e e e e e e

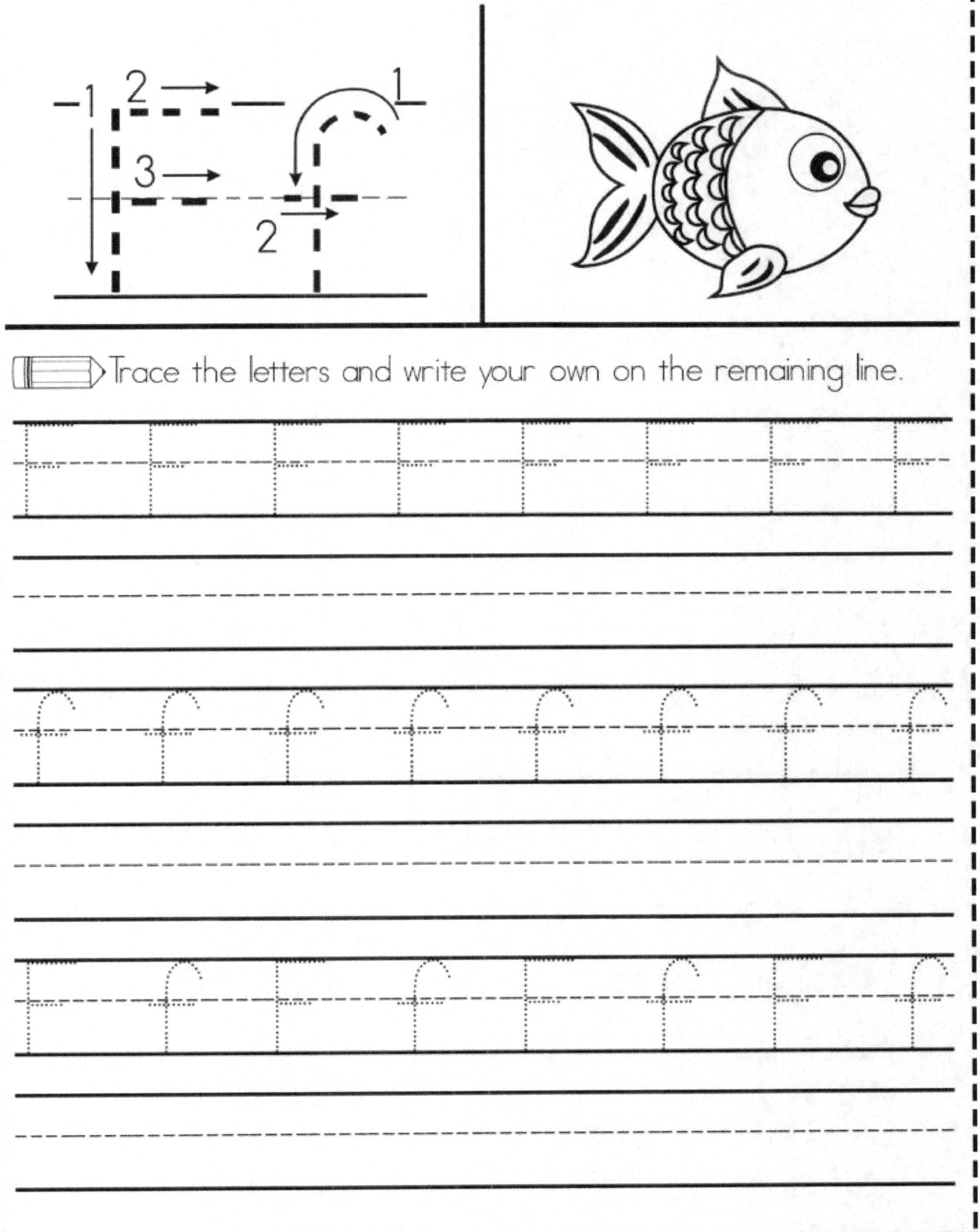

Trace the letters and write your own on the remaining line.

[illegible]

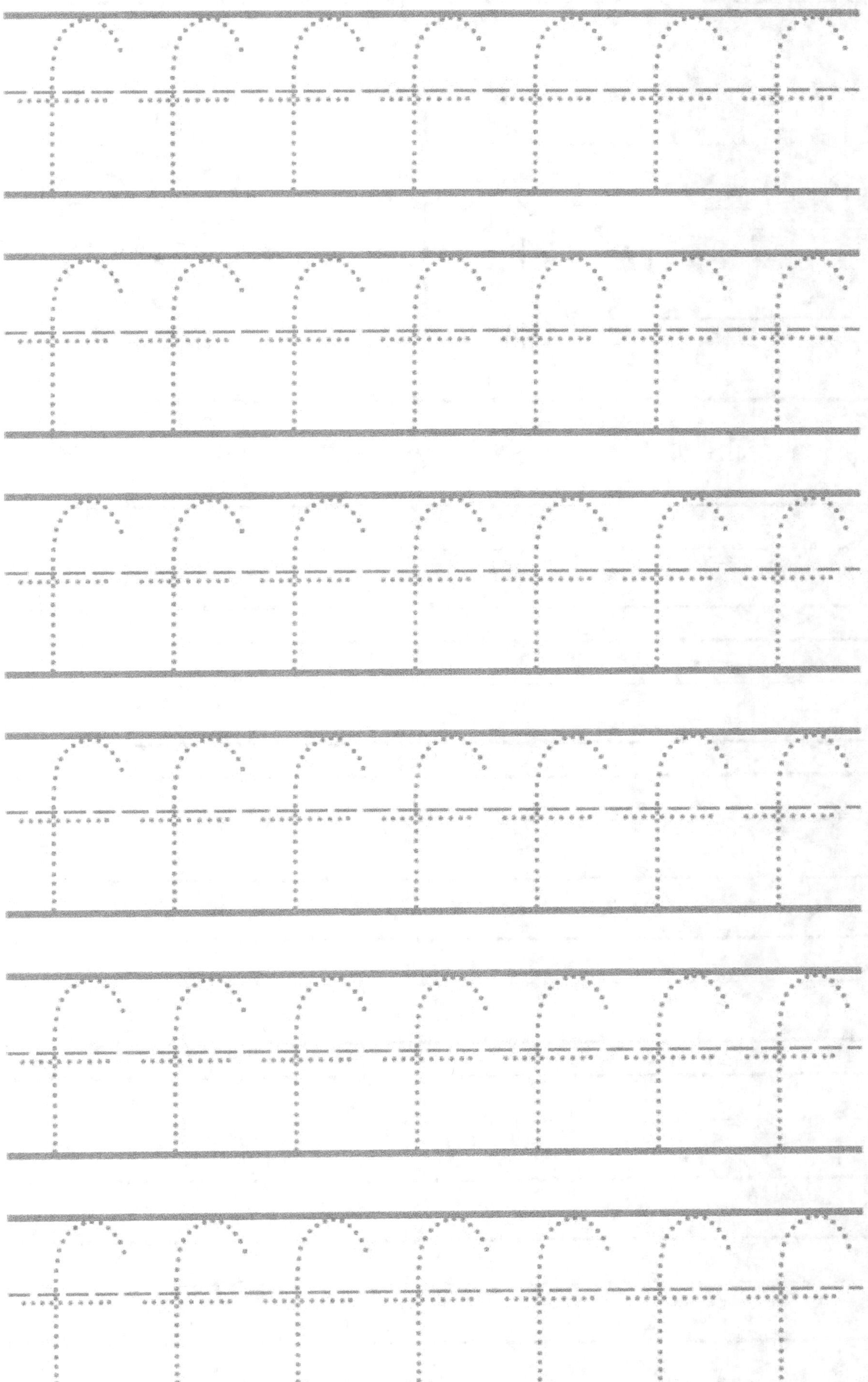

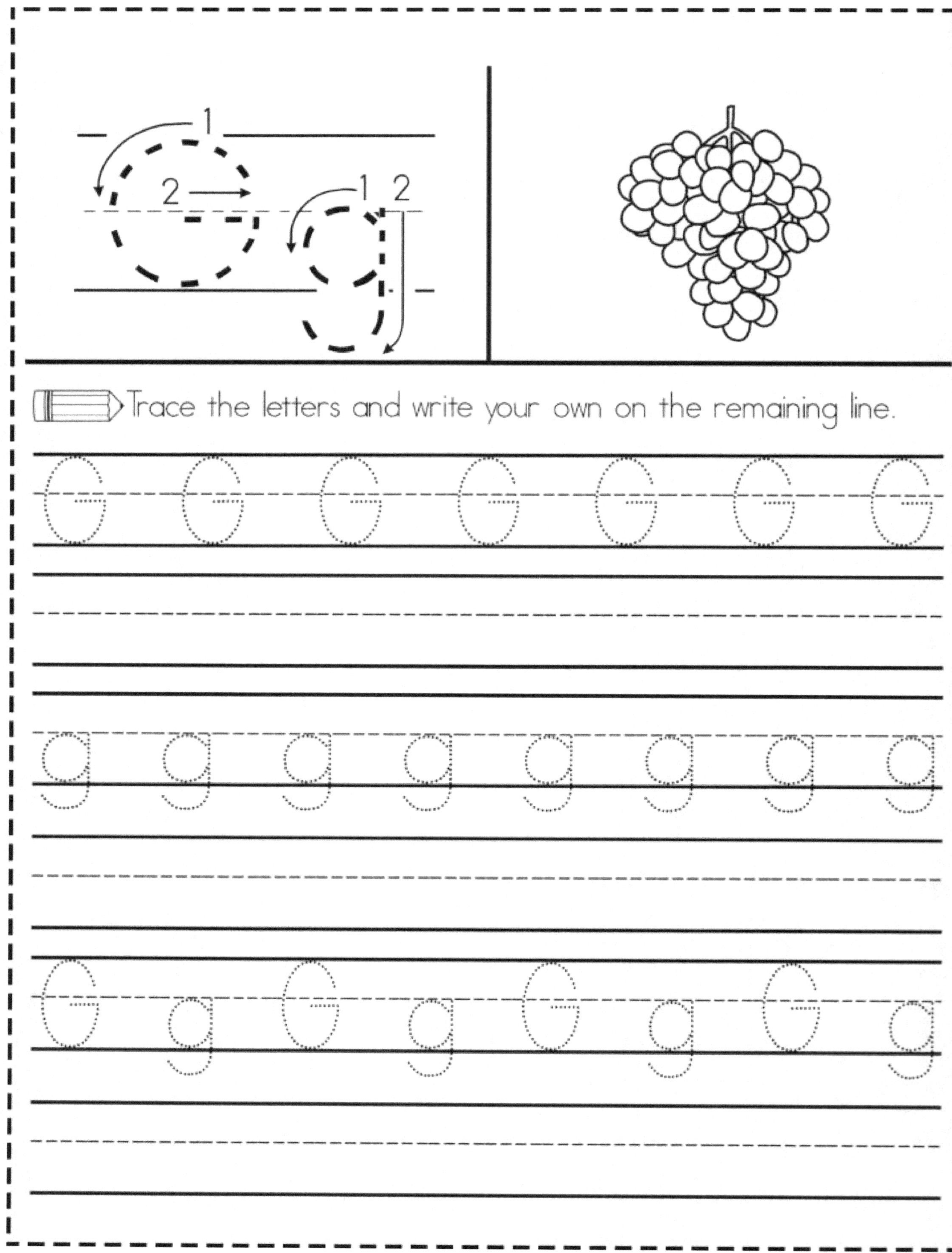

Trace the letters and write your own on the remaining line.

G G G G G G G

G G G G G G G

G G G G G G G

G G G G G G G

G G G G G G G

G G G G G G G

g g g g g g g

g g g g g g g

g g g g g g g

g g g g g g g

g g g g g g g

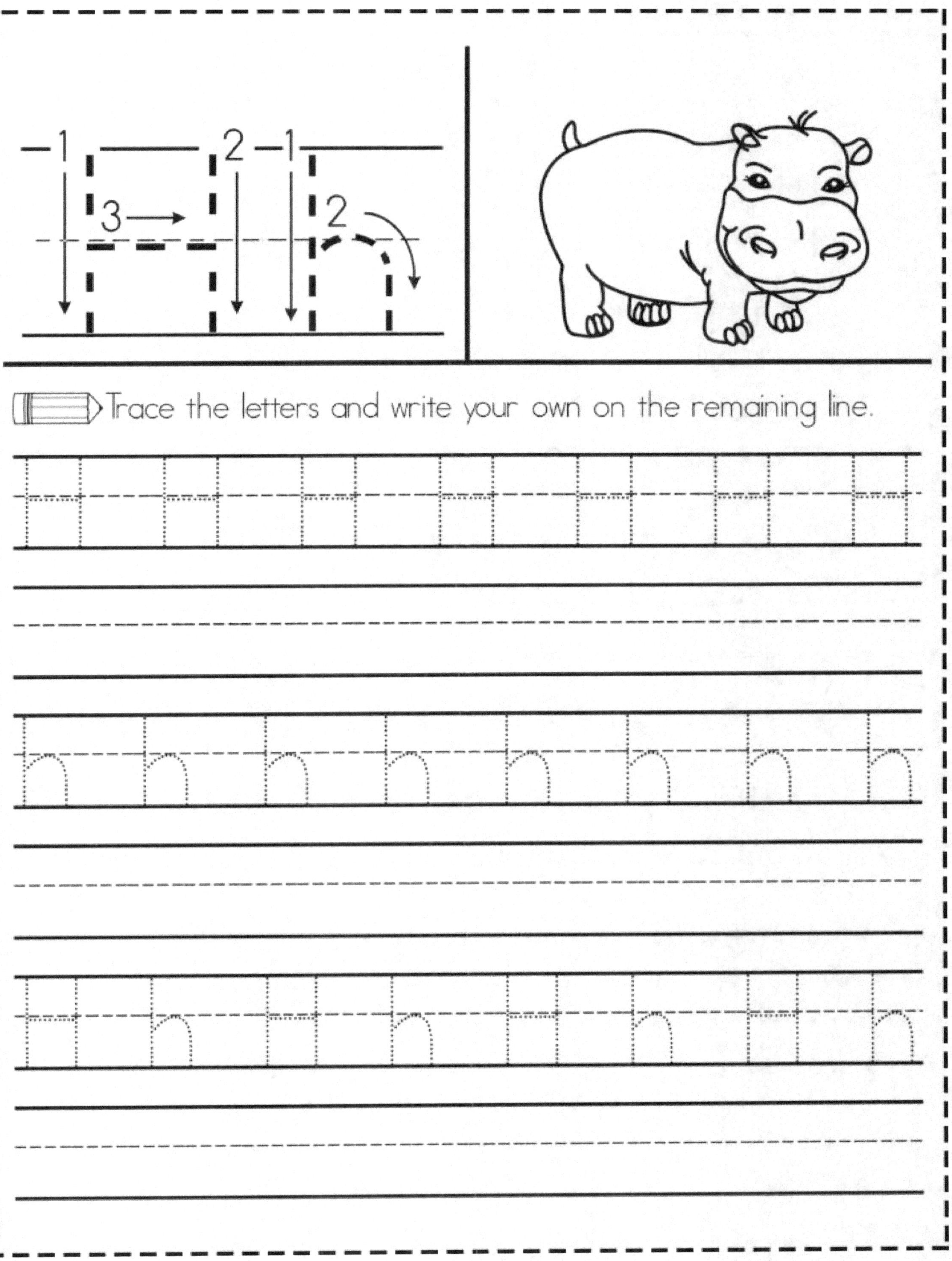

Trace the letters and write your own on the remaining line.

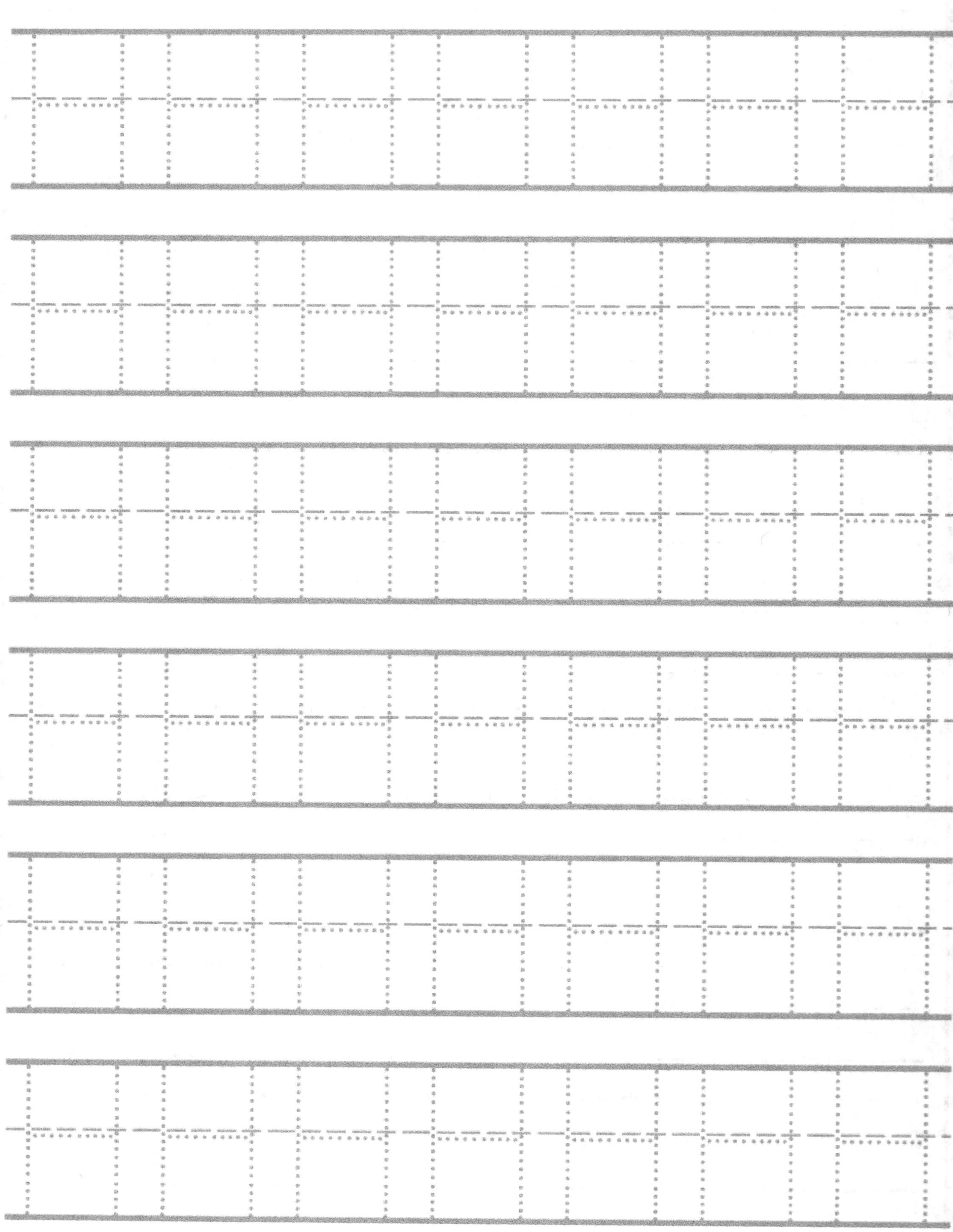

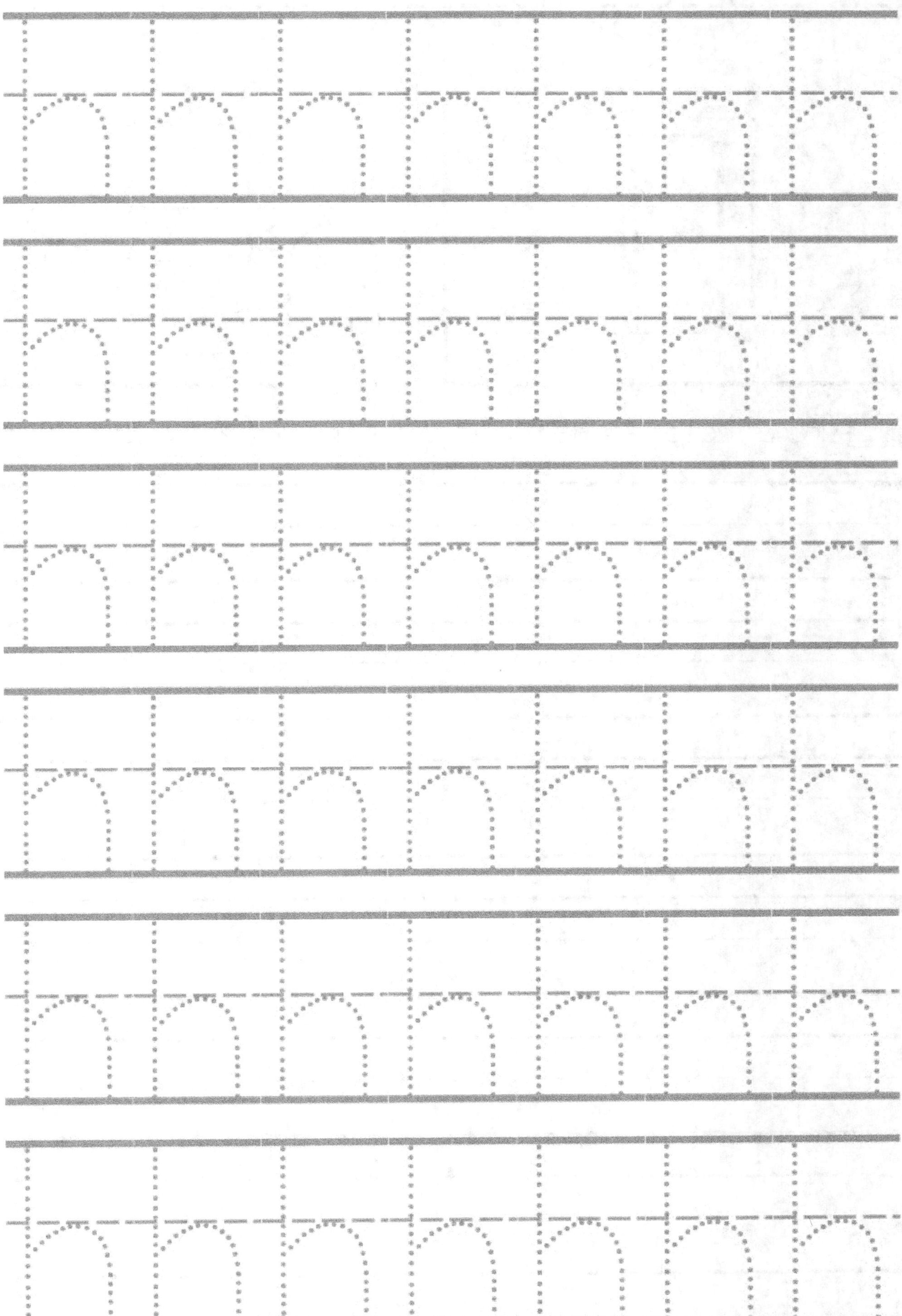

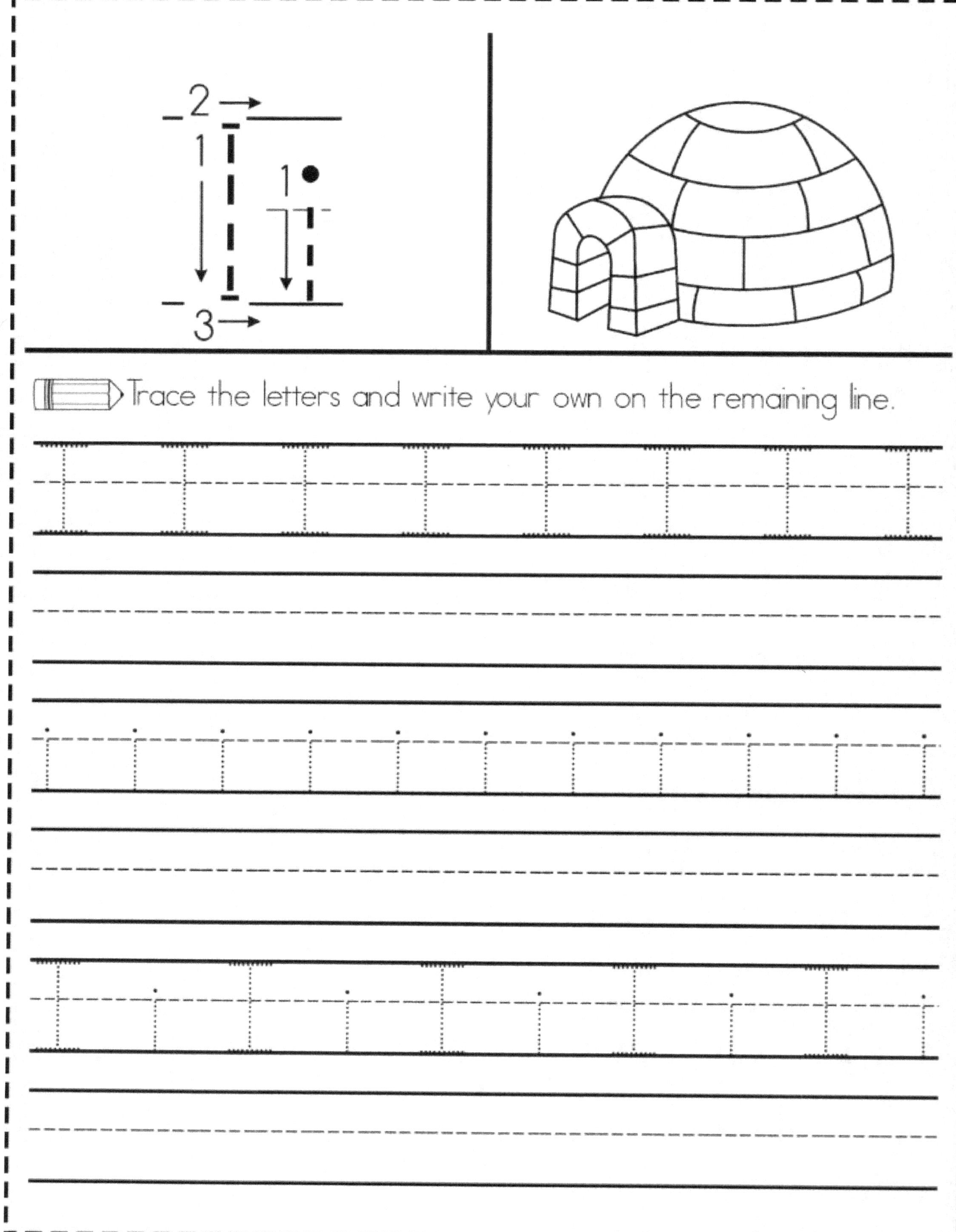

Trace the letters and write your own on the remaining line.

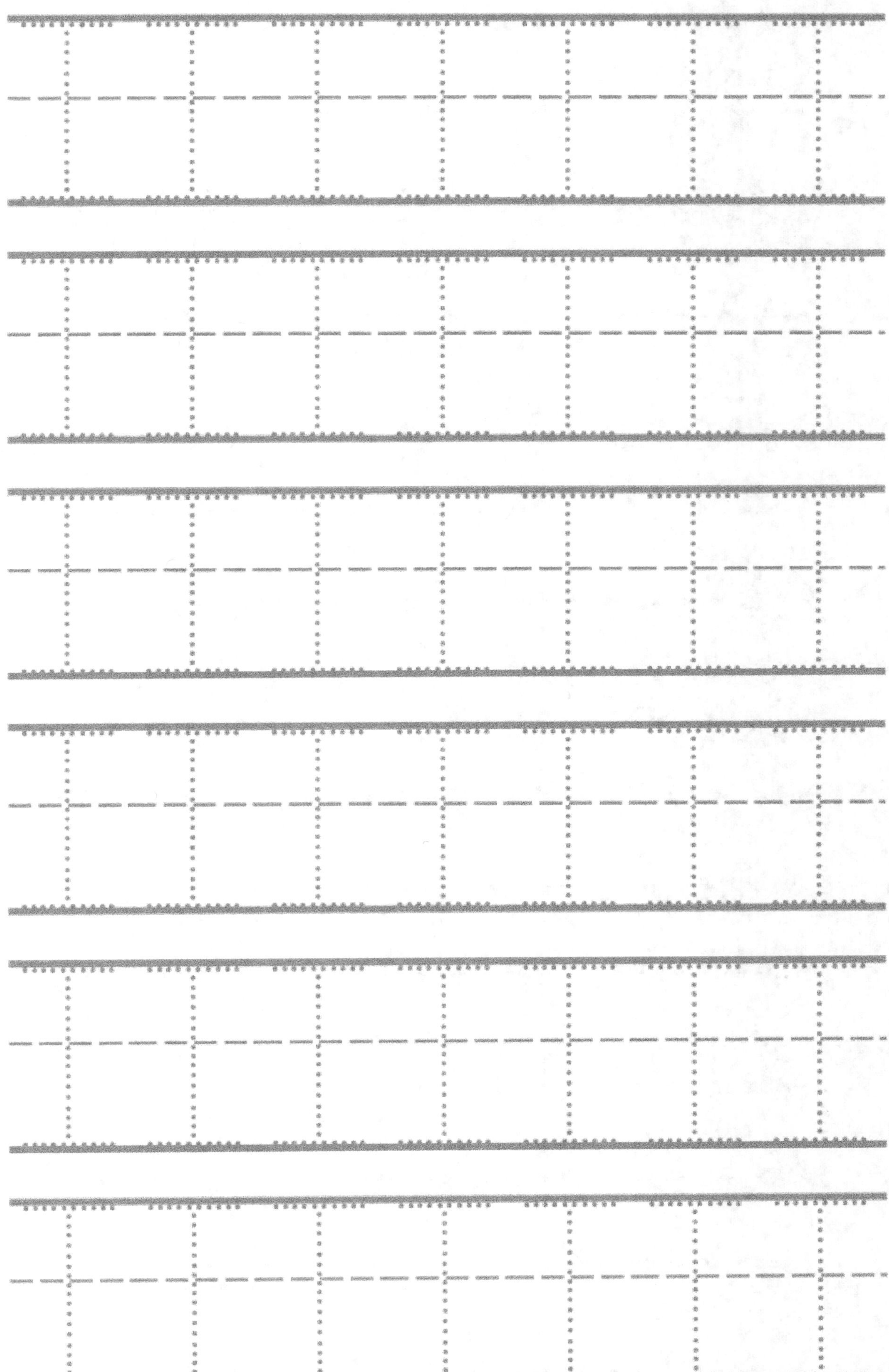

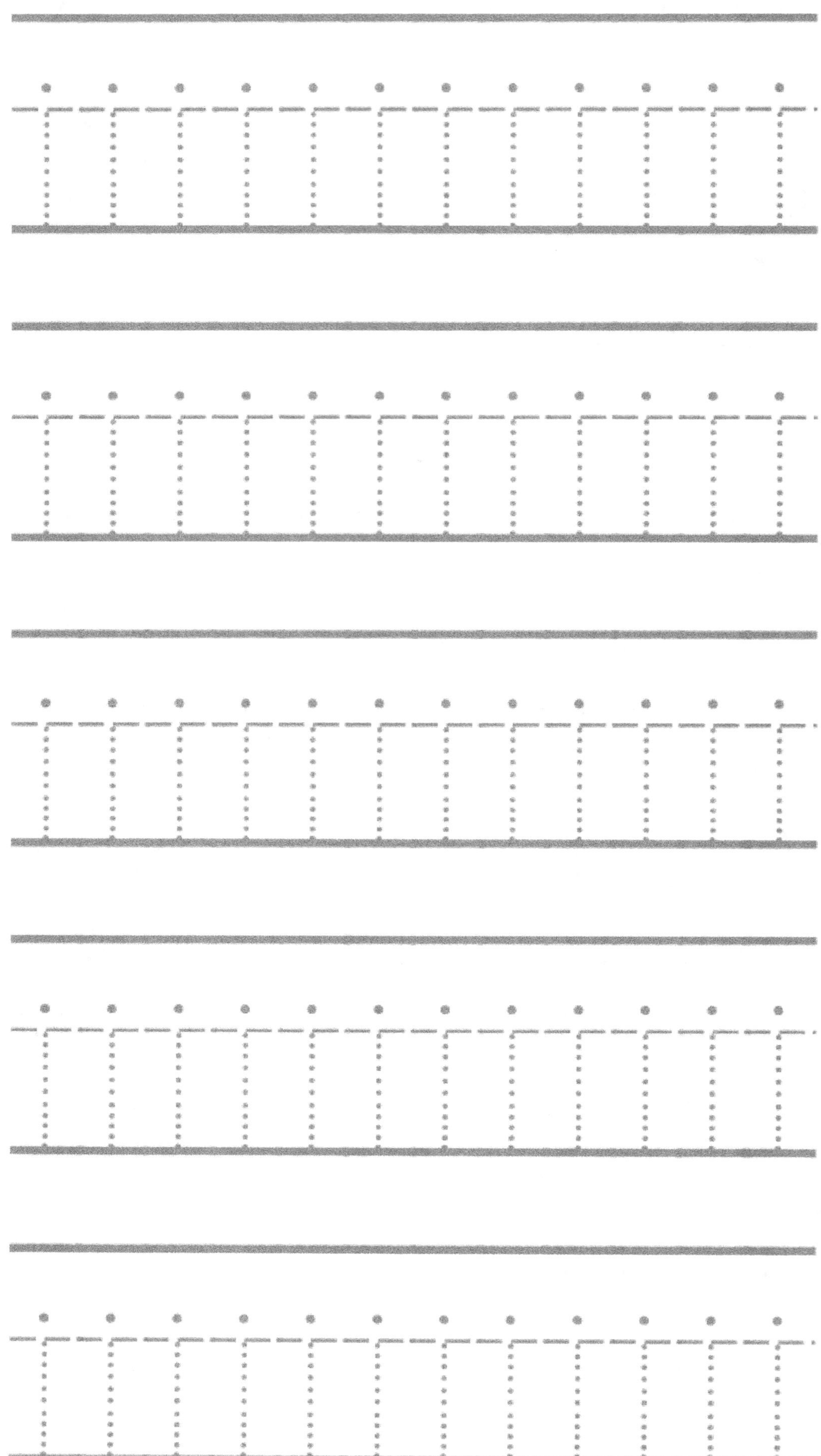

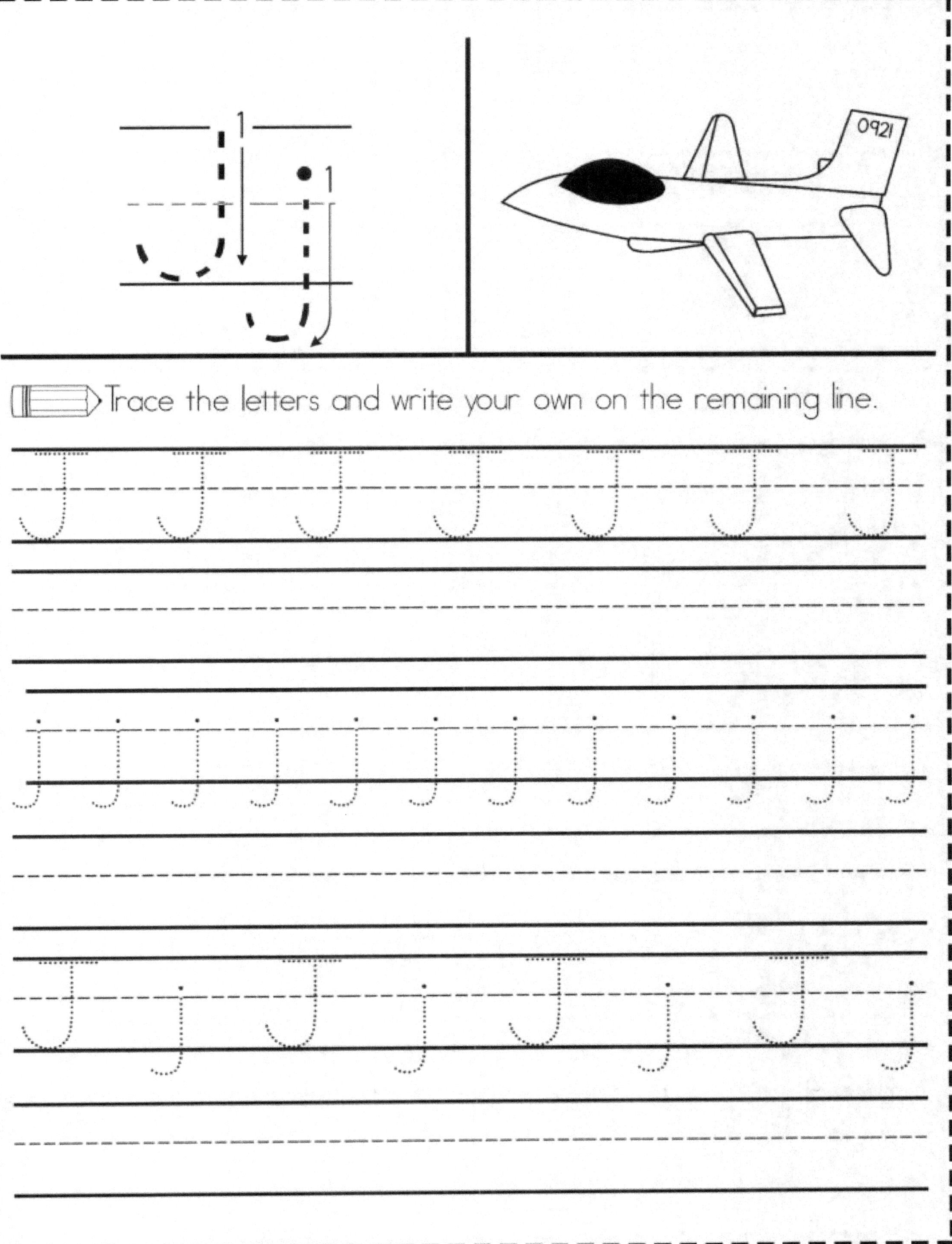

Trace the letters and write your own on the remaining line.

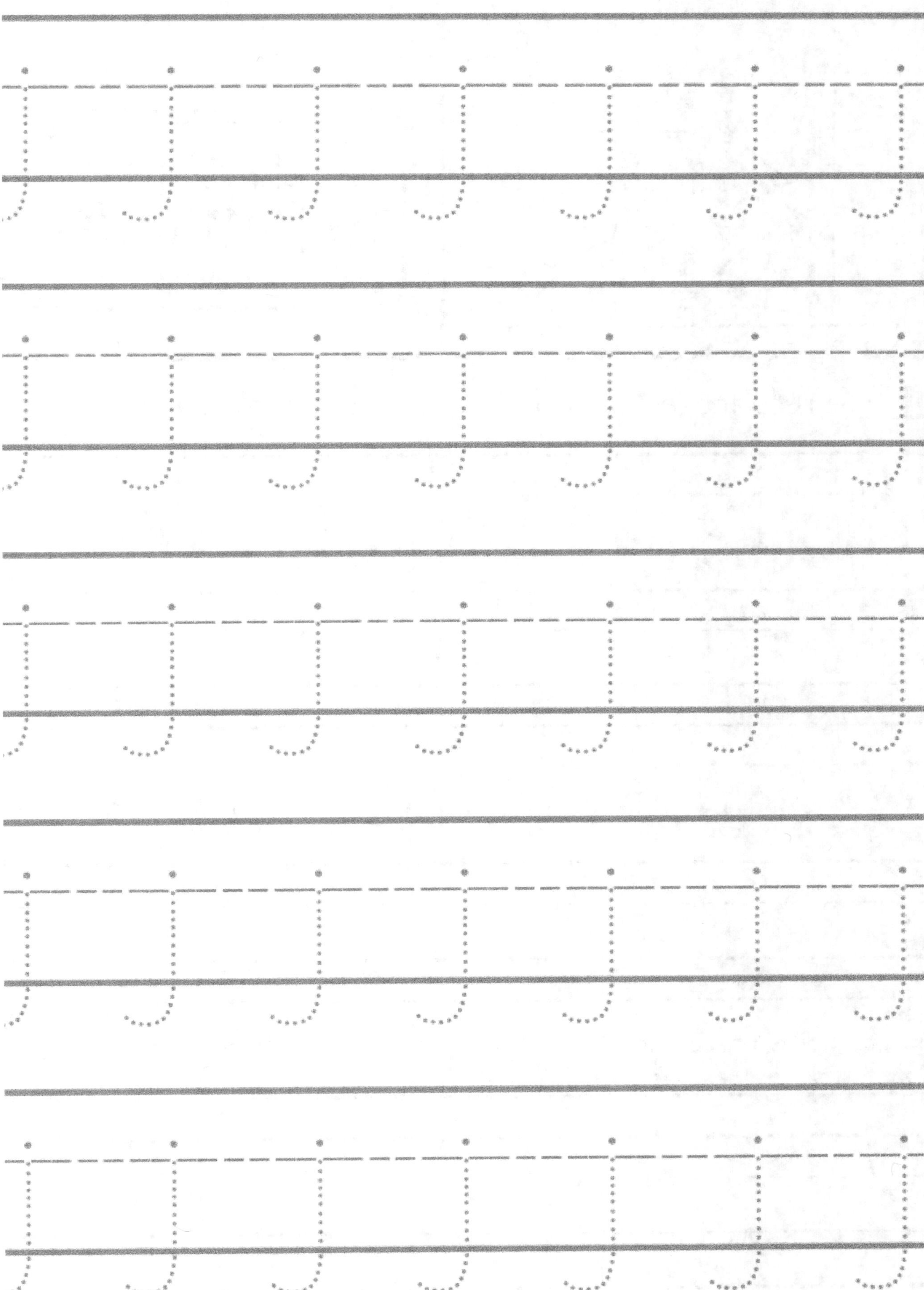

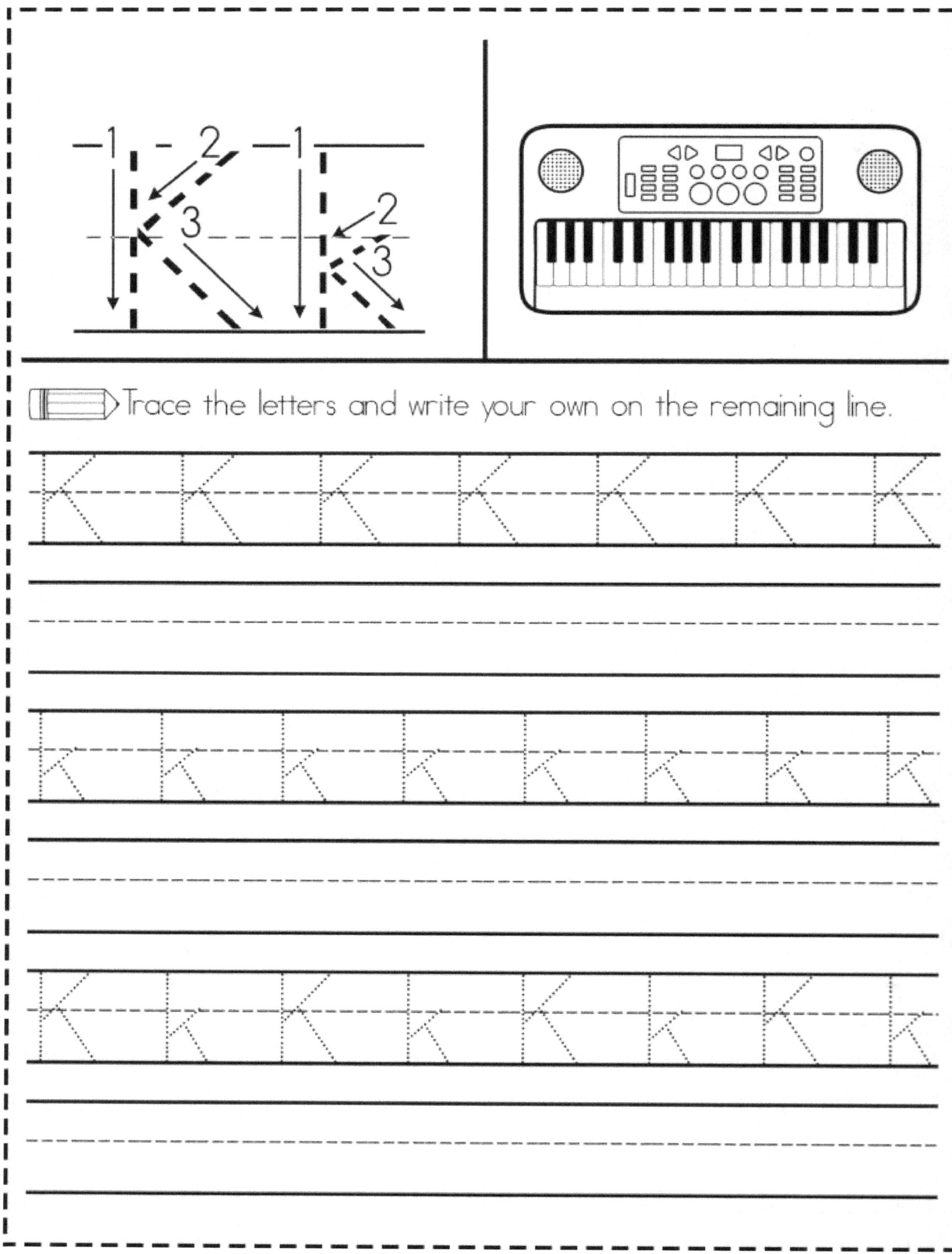

Trace the letters and write your own on the remaining line.

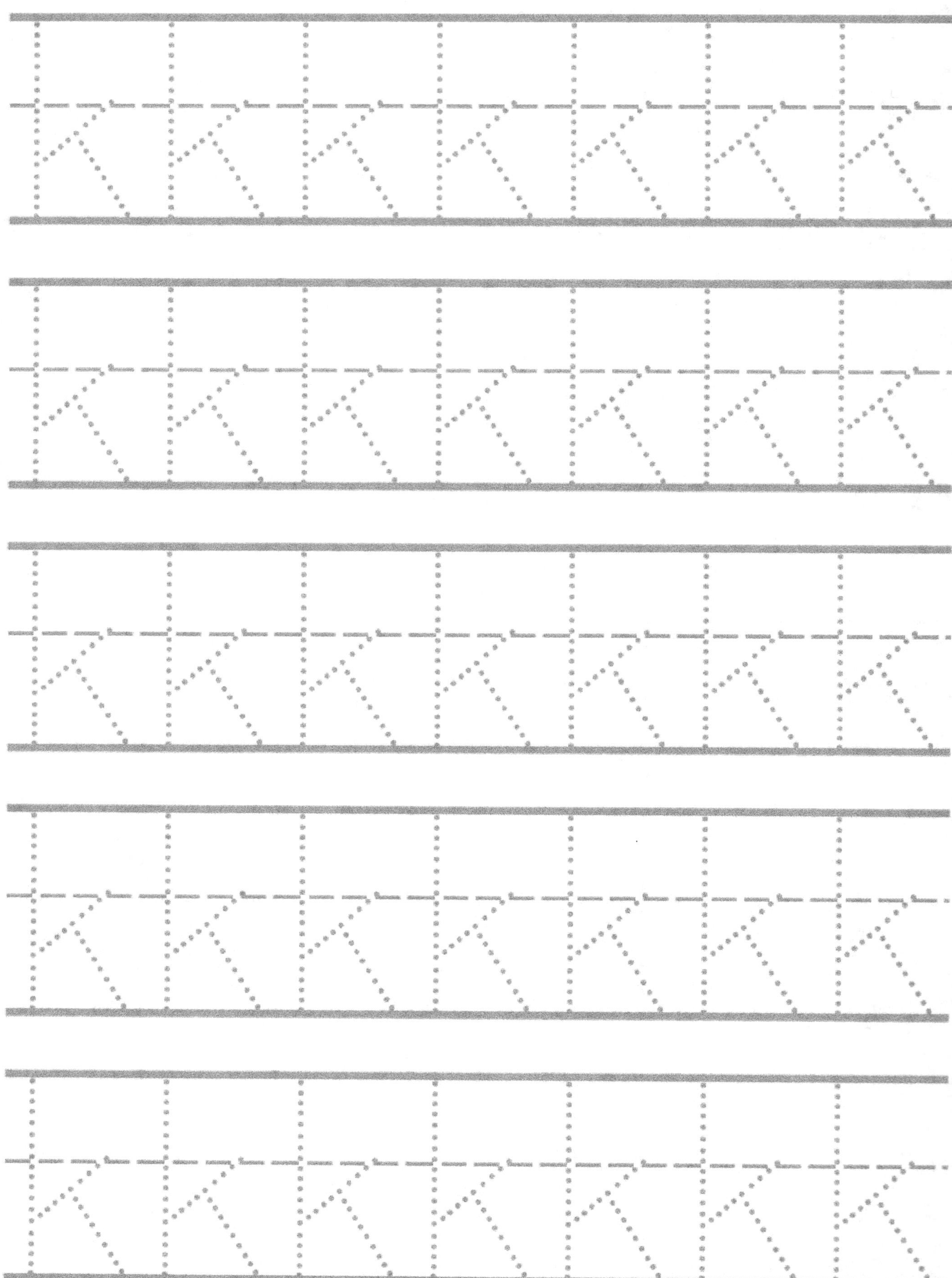

Trace the letters and write your own on the remaining line.

✏️ Trace the letters and write your own on the remaining line.

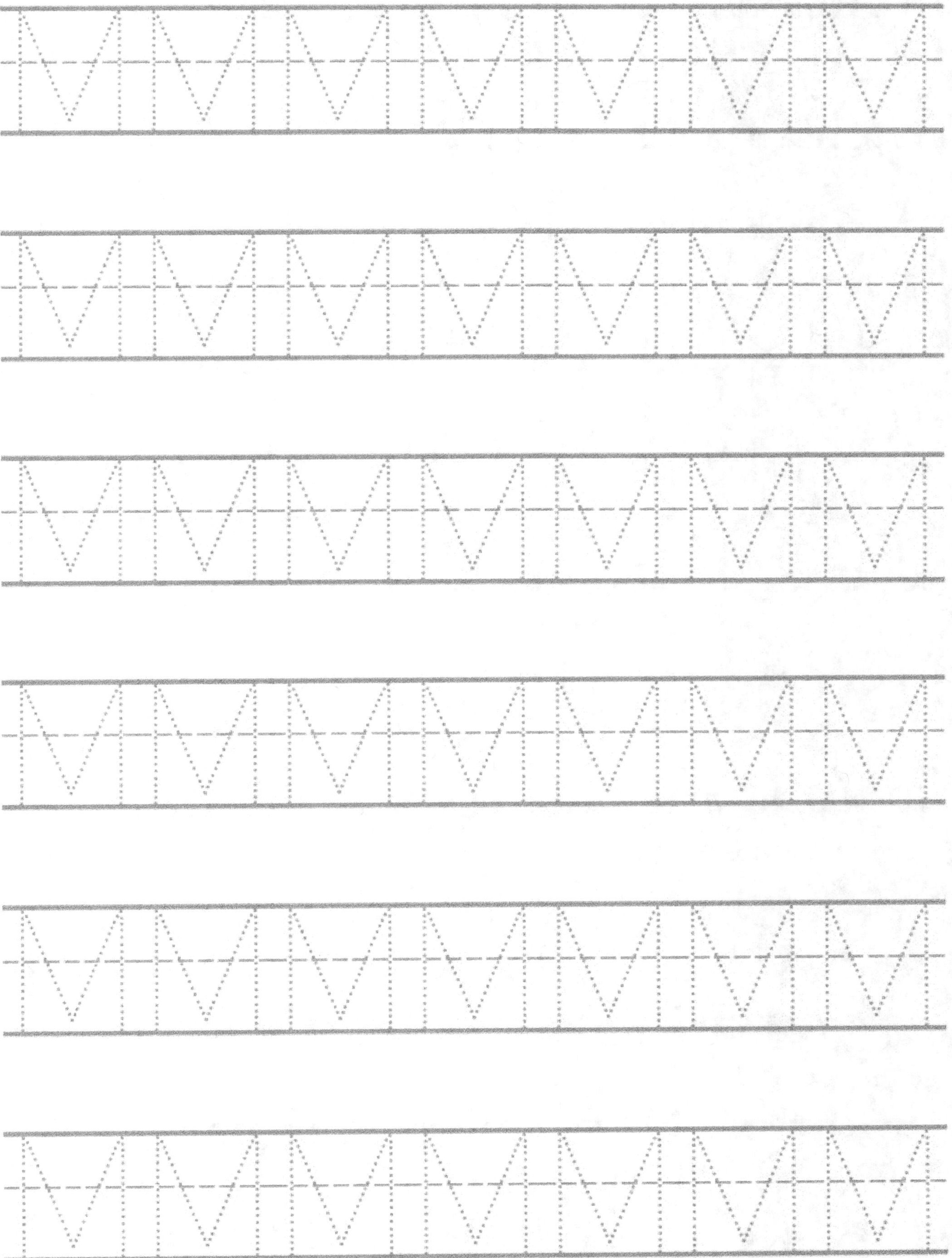

Trace the letters and write your own on the remaining line.

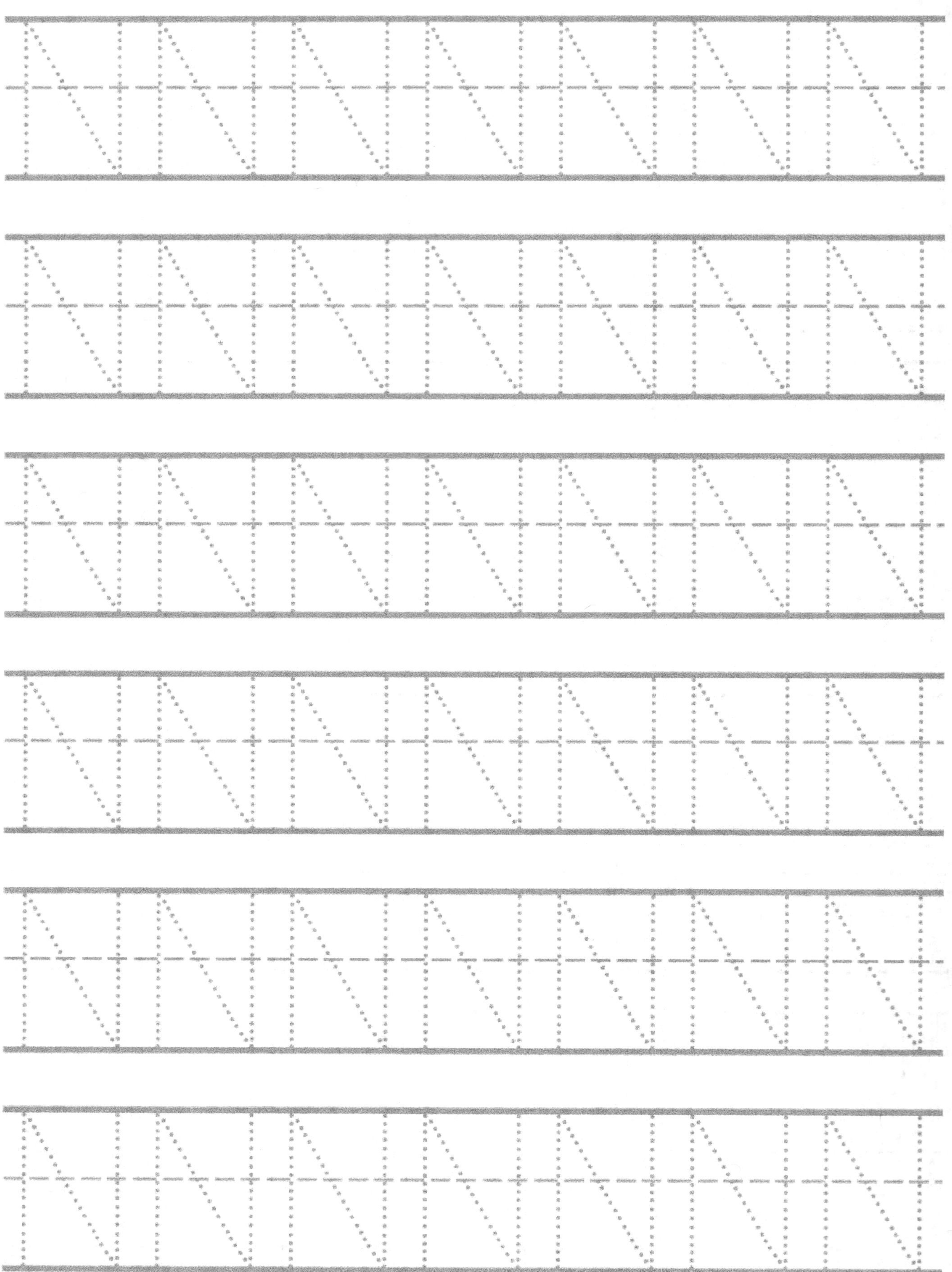

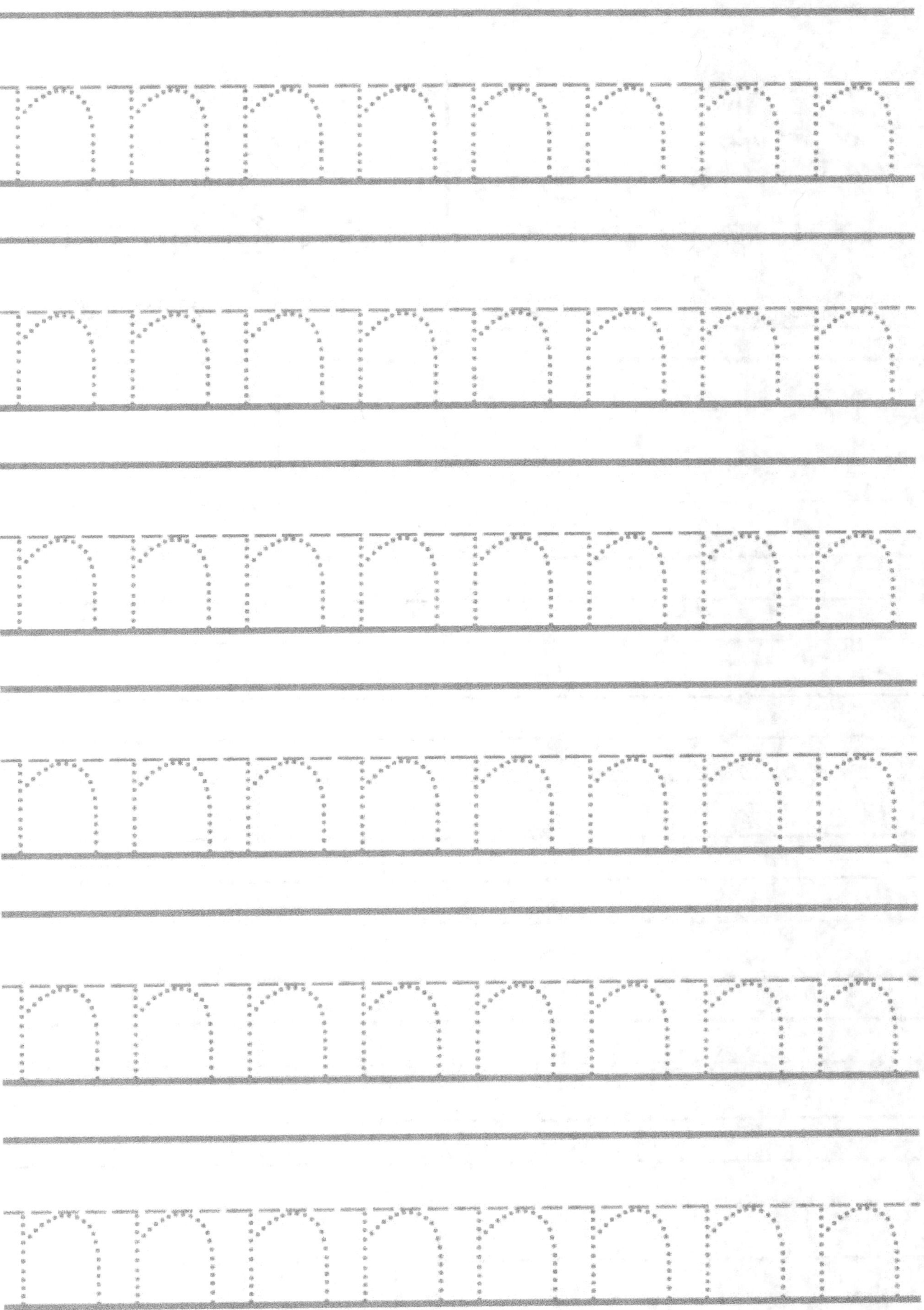

Trace the letters and write your own on the remaining line.

Trace the letters and write your own on the remaining line.

P P P P P P P P

p p p p p p p p

P p P p P p

p p p p p p p

p p p p p p p

p p p p p p p

p p p p p p p

p p p p p p p

p p p p p p p

p p p p p p p

p p p p p p p

p p p p p p p

p p p p p p p

p p p p p p p

p p p p p p p

p p p p p p p

p p p p p p p

p p p p p p p

Trace the letters and write your own on the remaining line.

a a a a a a a a

a a a a a a a a

a a a a a a a a

a a a a a a a a

a a a a a a a a

a a a a a a a a

Trace the letters and write your own on the remaining line.

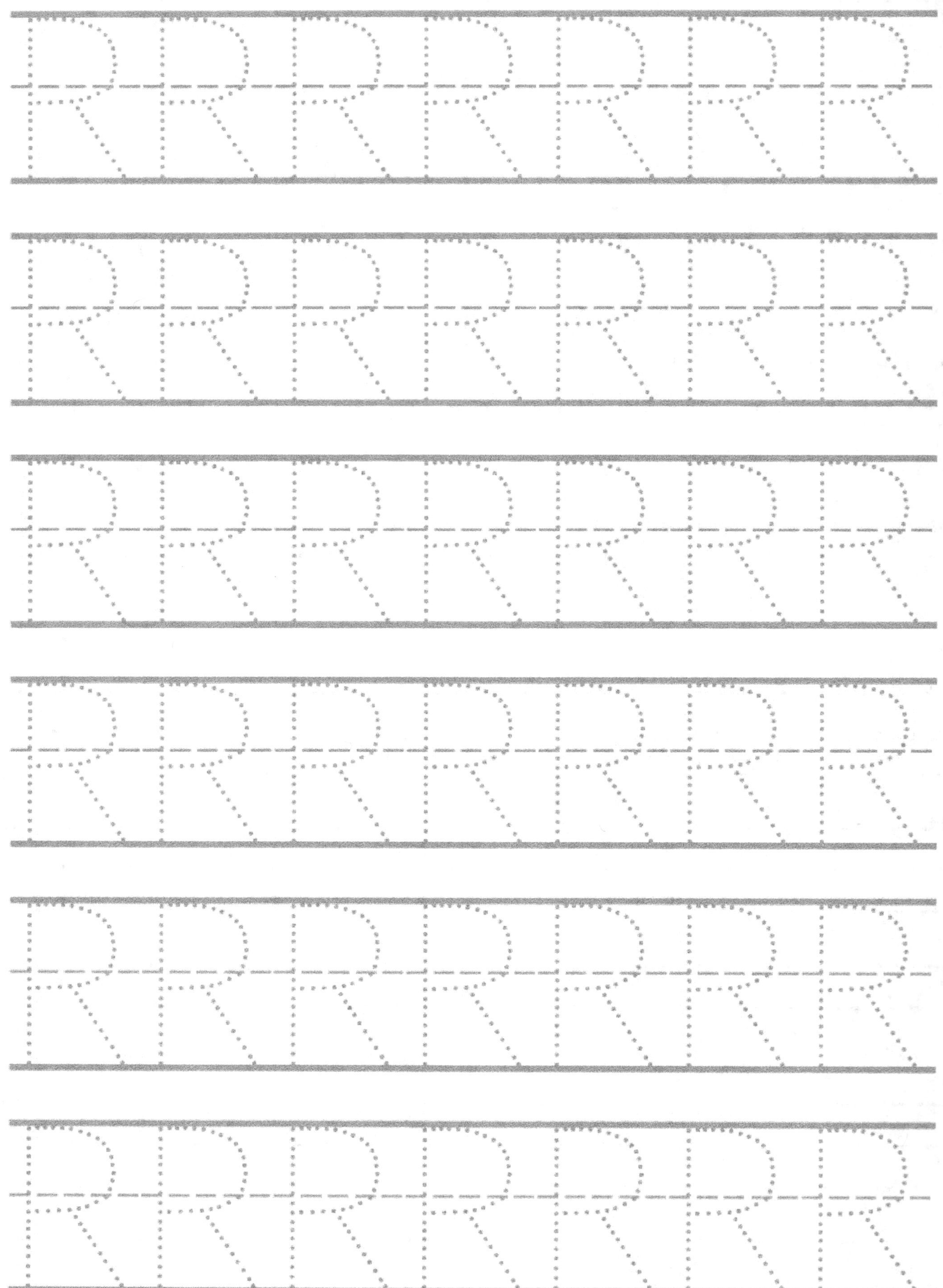

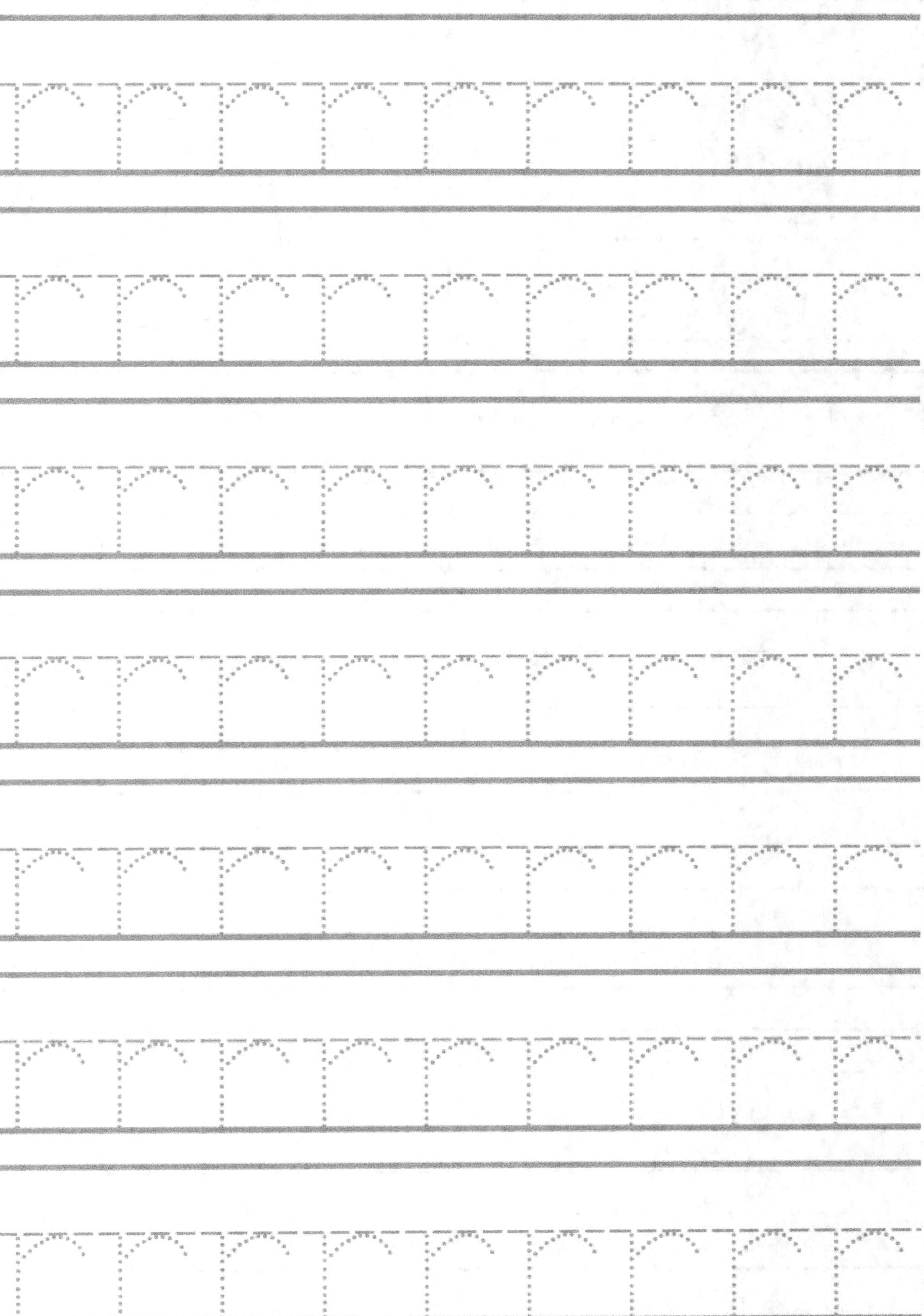

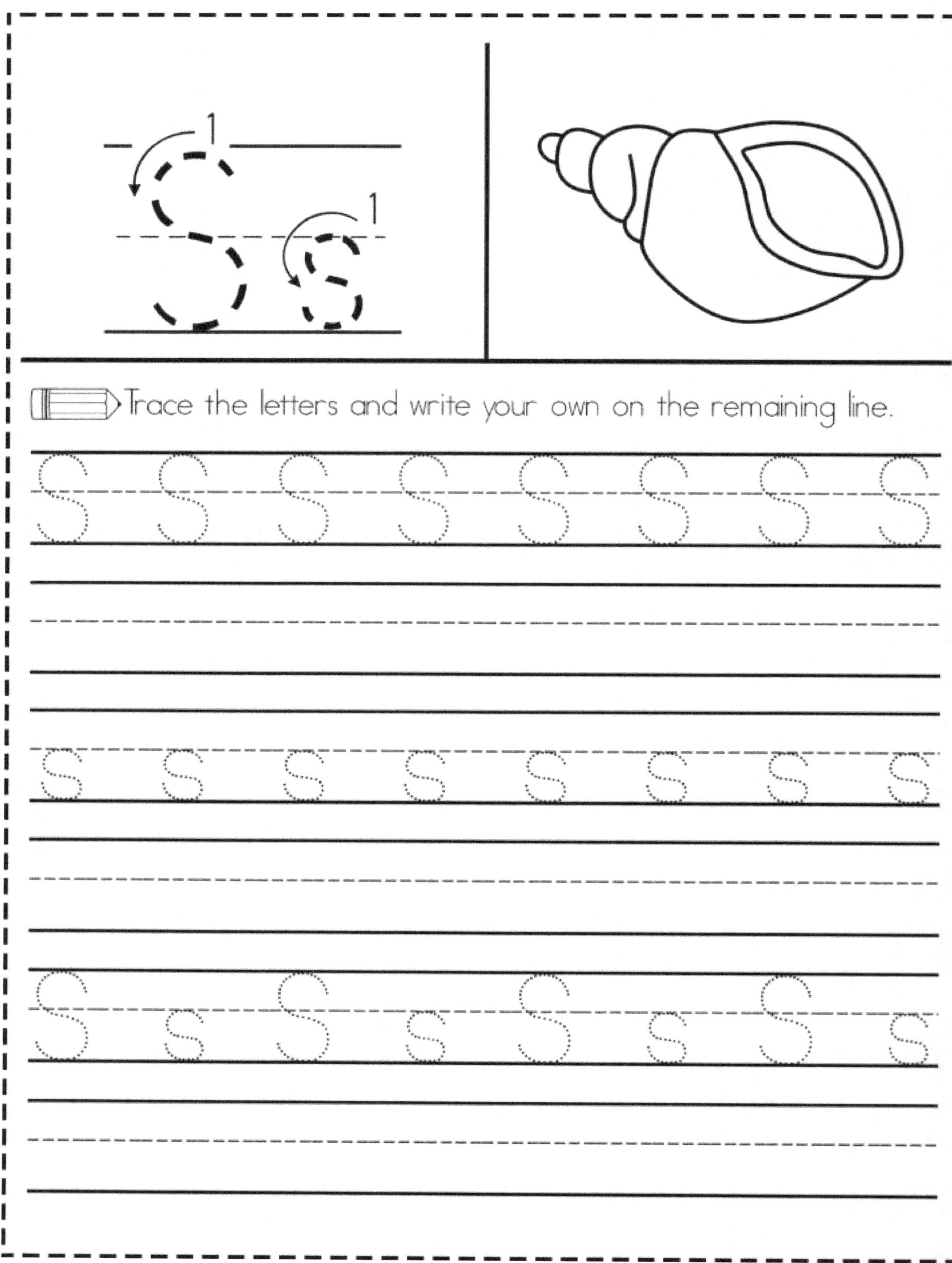

1
1
Trace the letters and write your own on the remaining line.

S S S S S S S S

S S S S S S S S

S S S S S S S S

S S S S S S S S

S S S S S S S S

S S S S S S S S

S S S S S S S S S

S S S S S S S S S

S S S S S S S S S

S S S S S S S S S

S S S S S S S S S

S S S S S S S S S

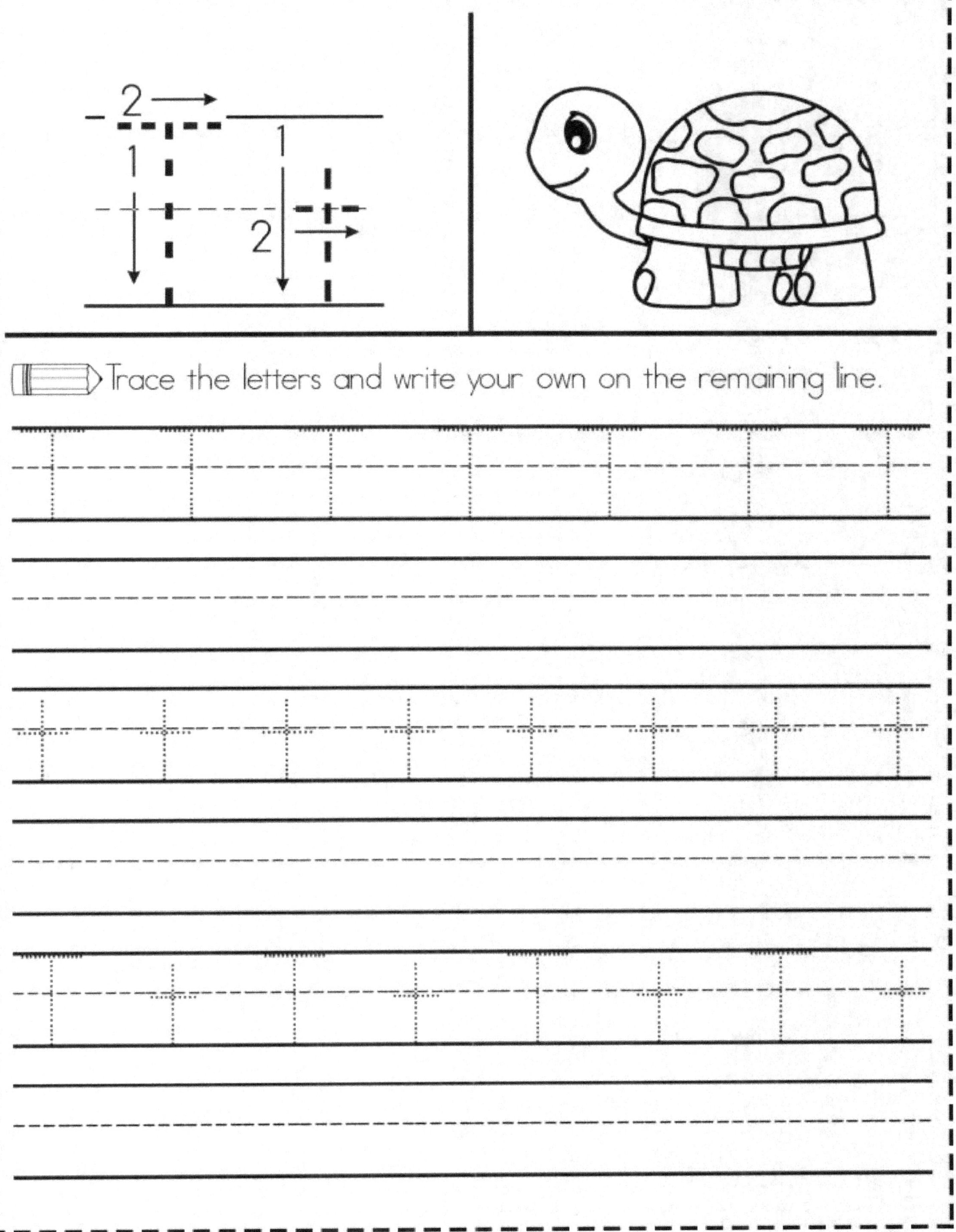

Trace the letters and write your own on the remaining line.

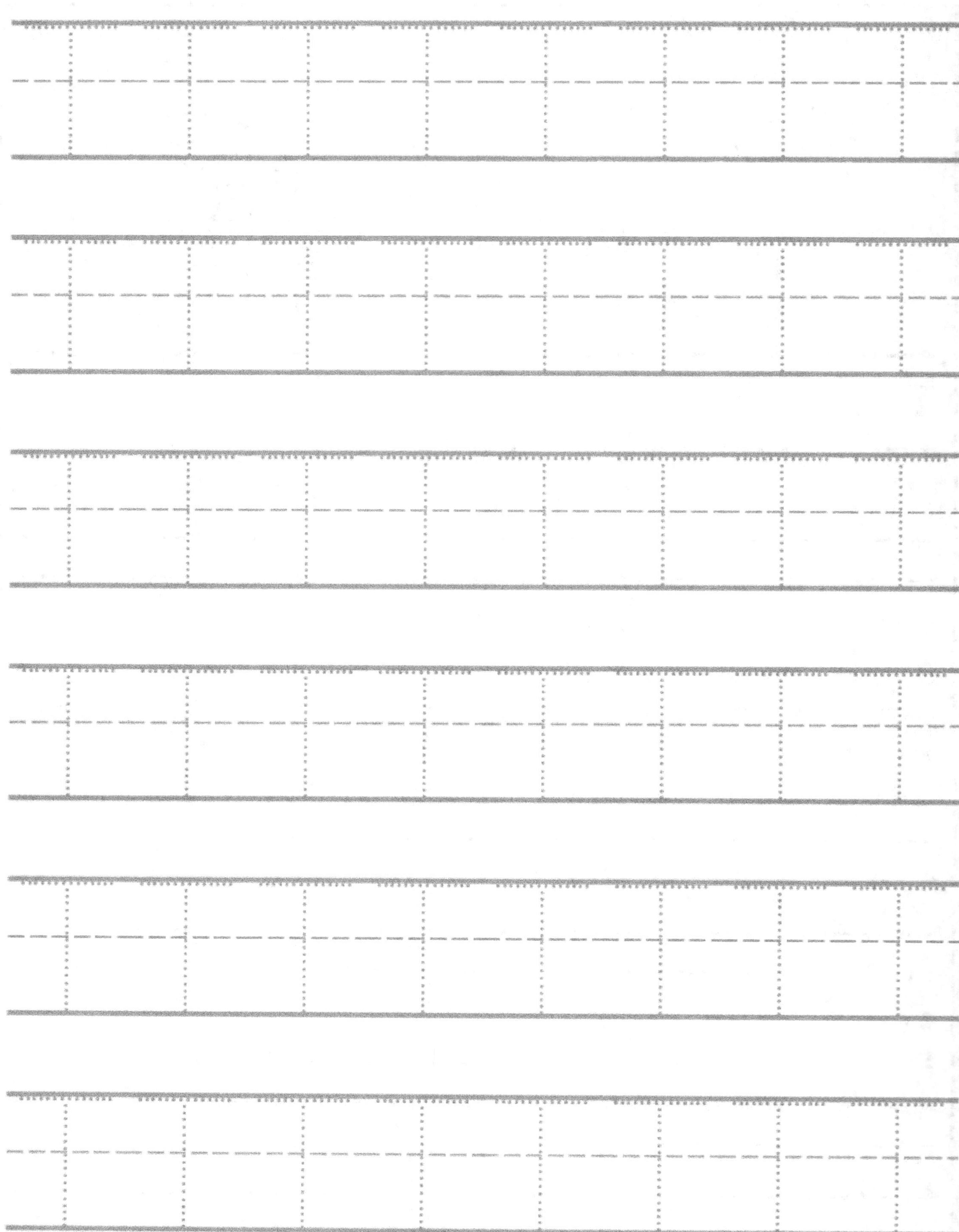

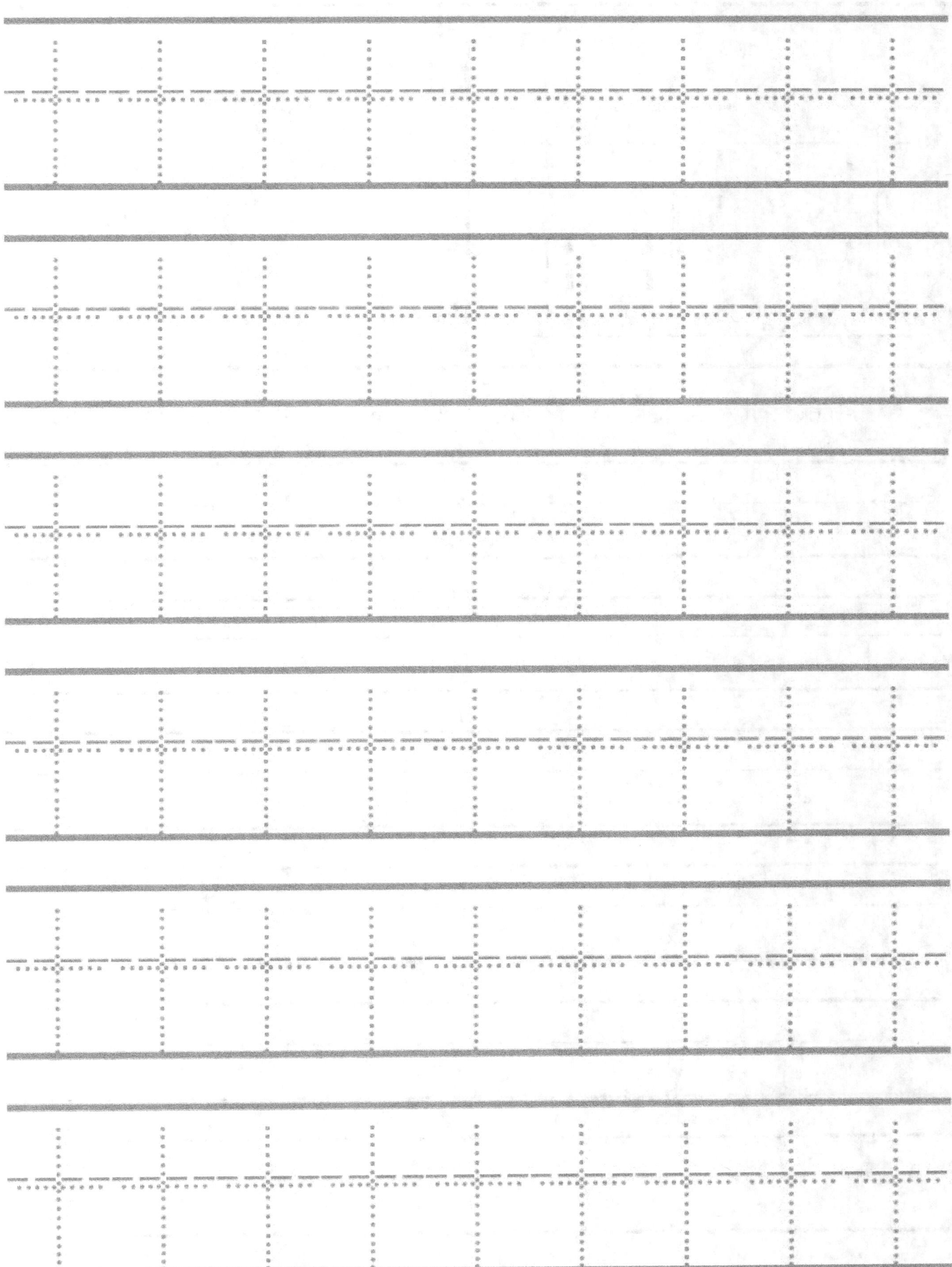

Trace the letters and write your own on the remaining line.

Trace the letters and write your own on the remaining line.

-1 -2 3 - 4
1 2 3 4
Trace the letters and write your own on the remaining line.

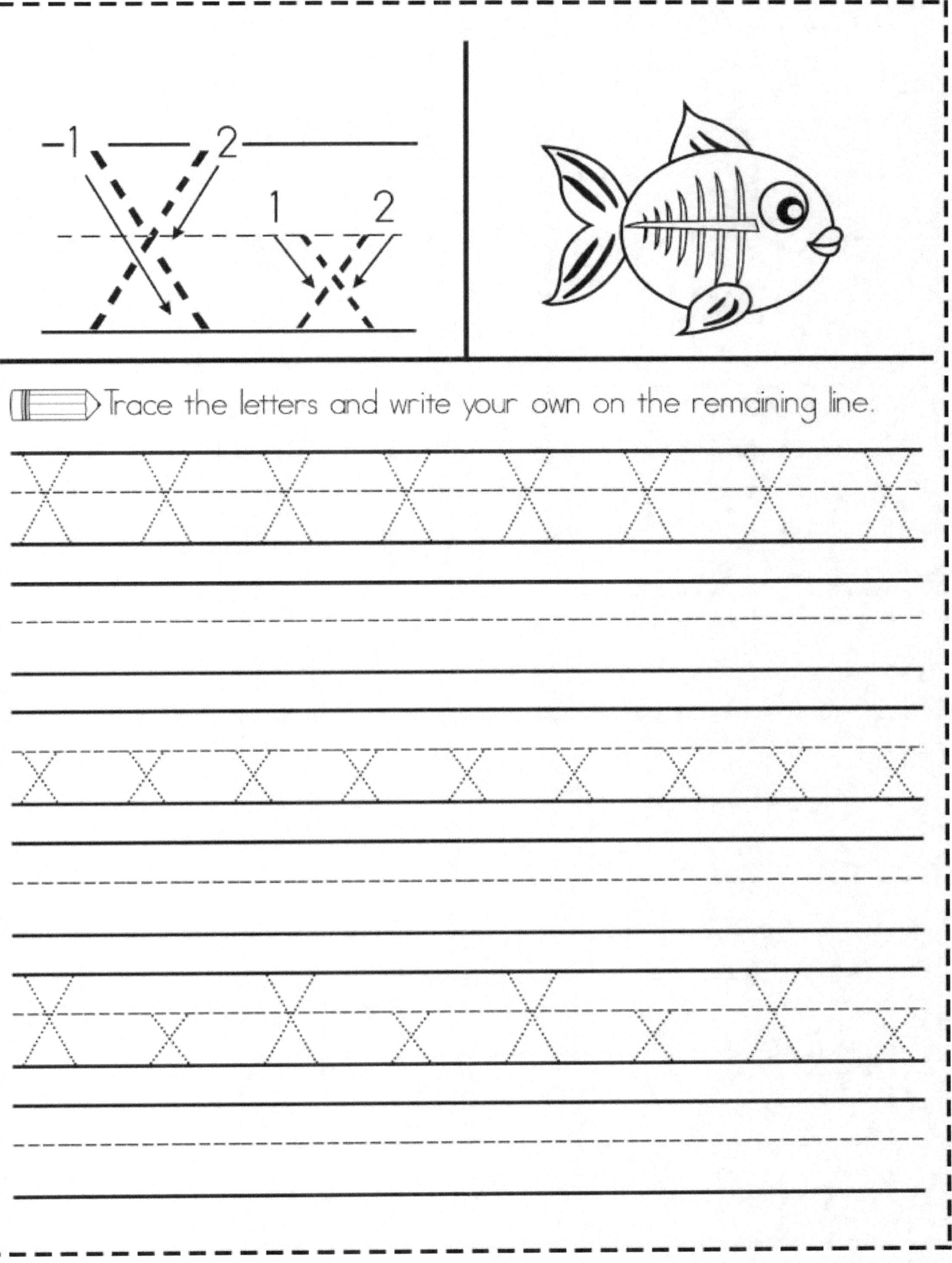

-1
2
1
2
Trace the letters and write your own on the remaining line.

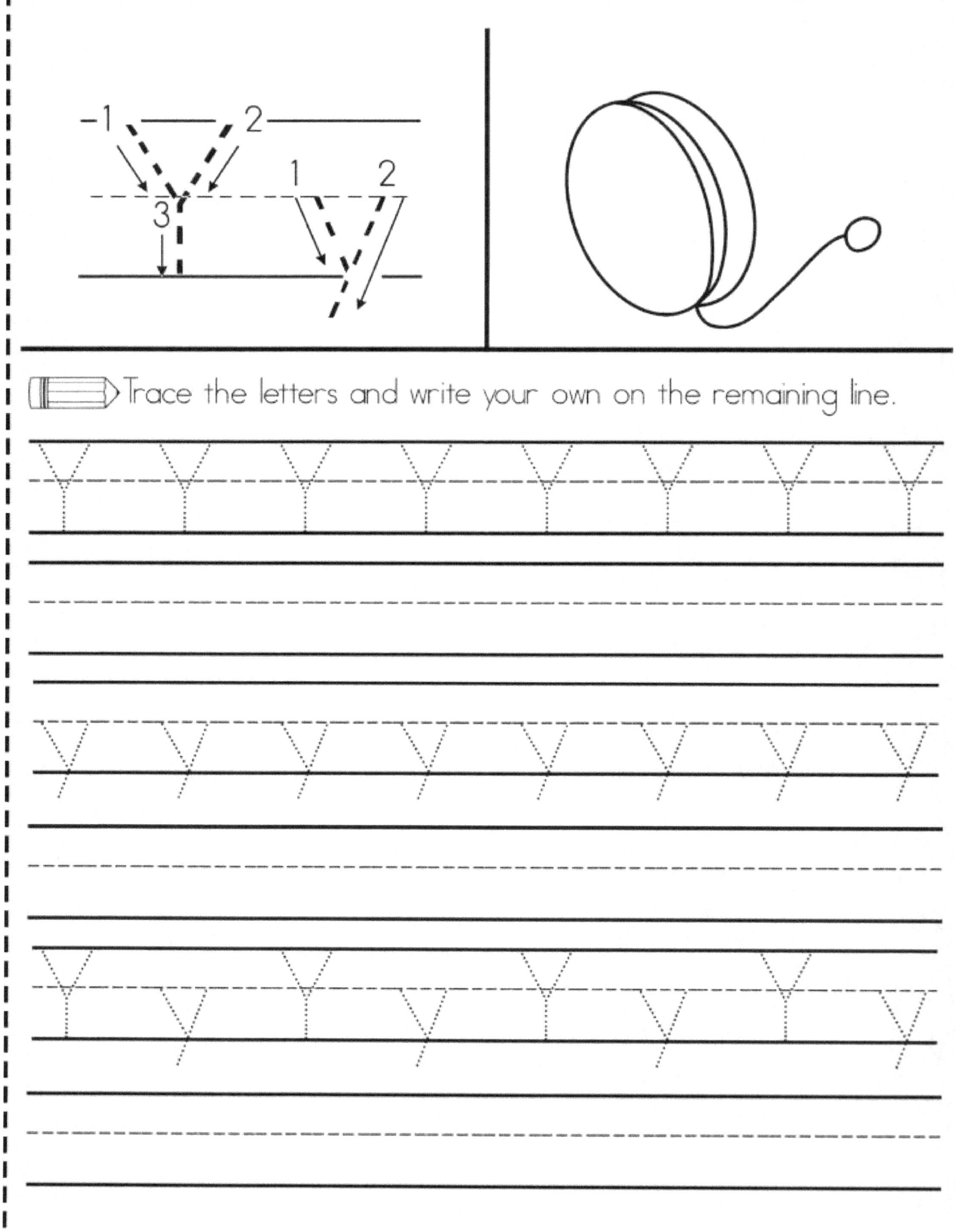

Trace the letters and write your own on the remaining line.

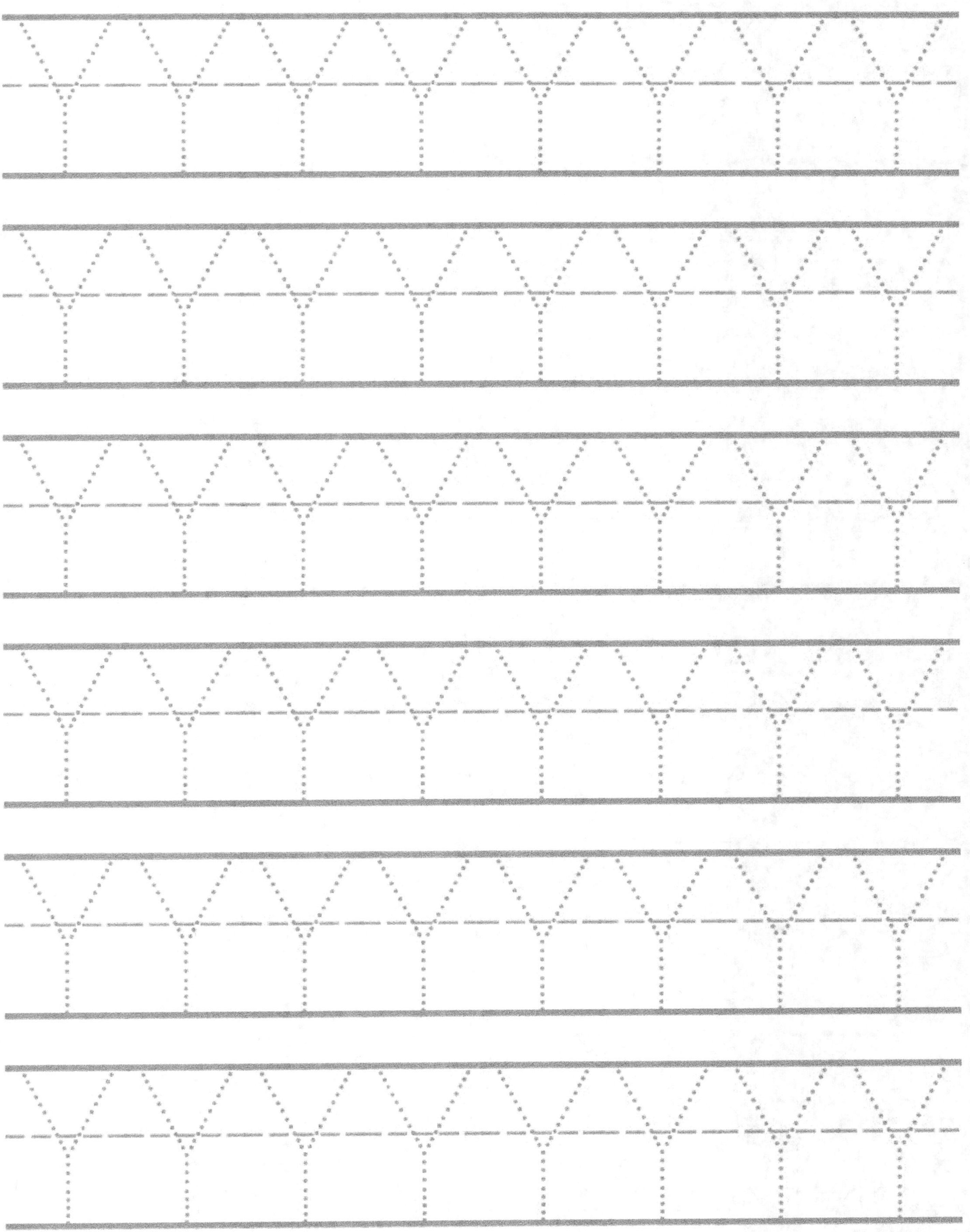

Trace the letters and write your own on the remaining line.

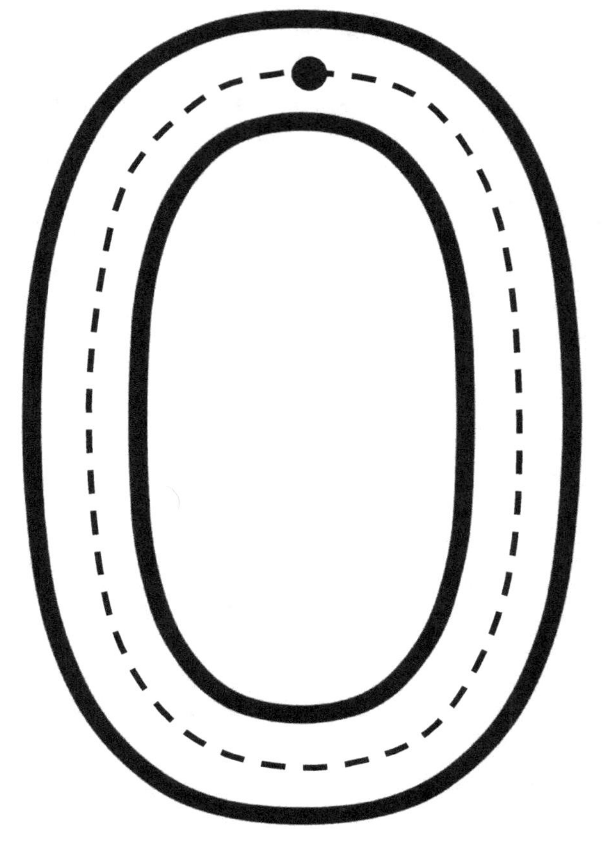

ZERO

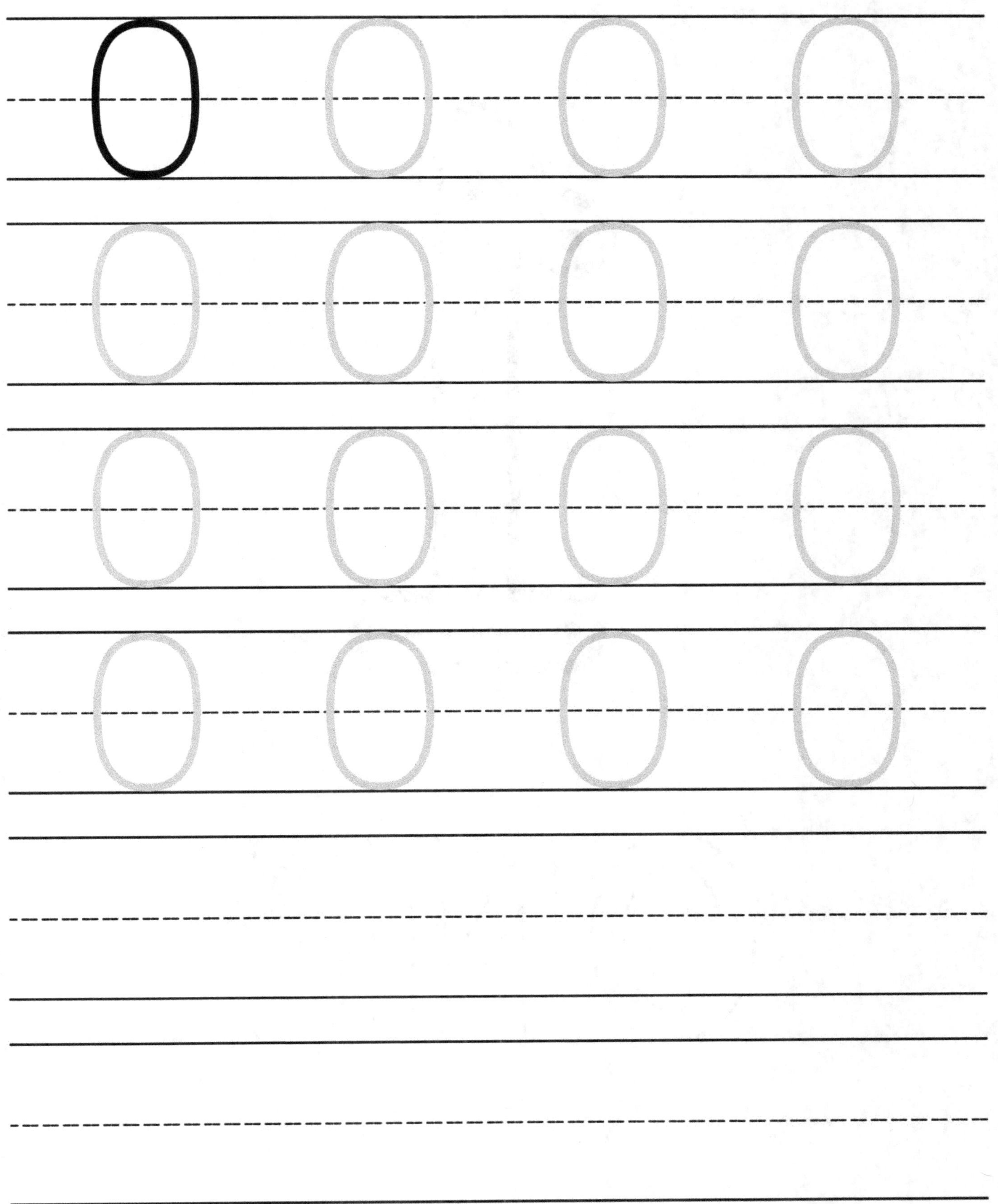

ONE

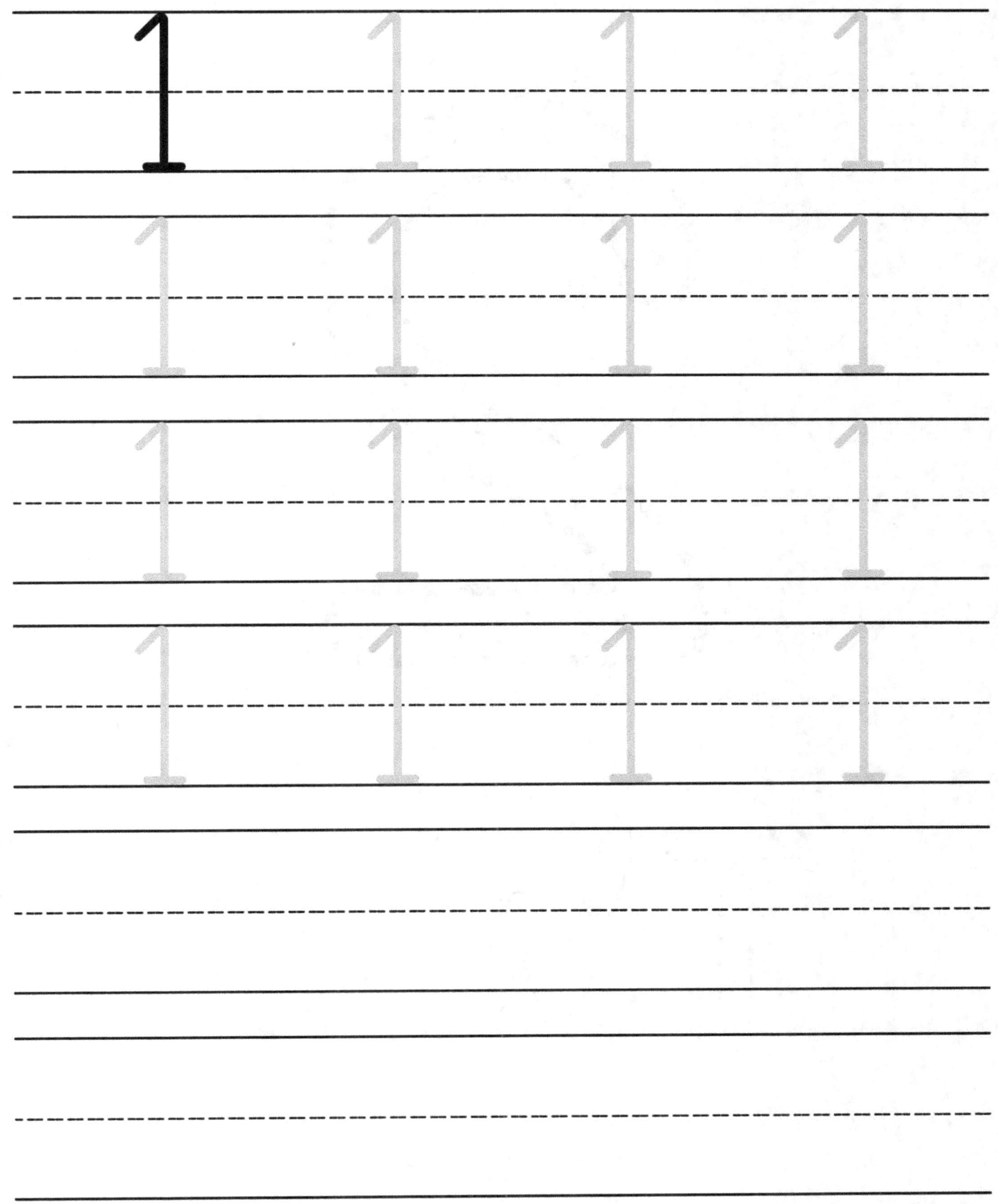

TWO

2

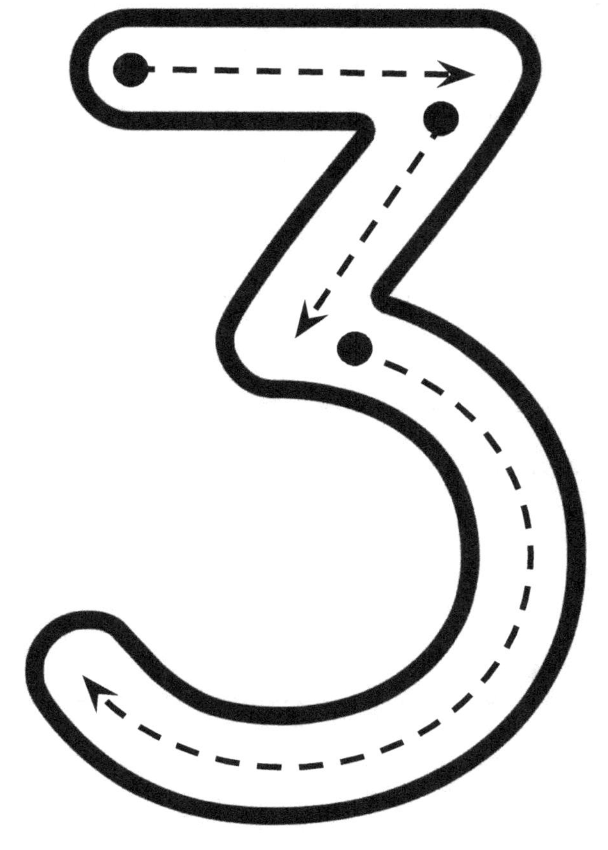

THREE

3 3 3 3

3 3 3 3

3 3 3 3

3 3 3 3

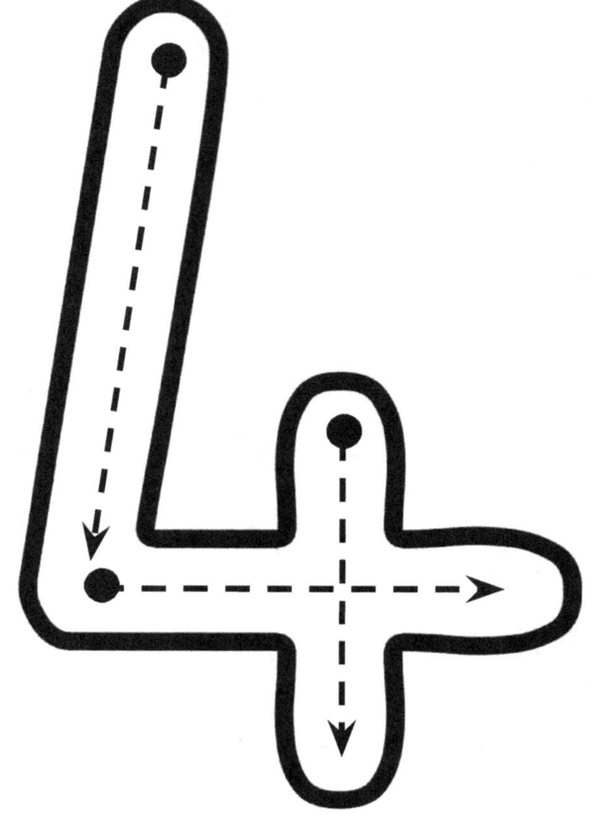

FOUR

4

FIVE

5

SIX

6

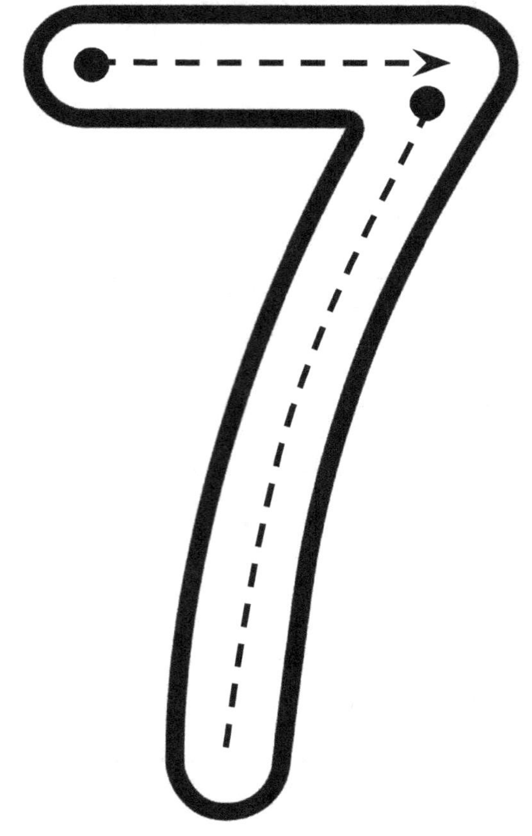

SEVEN

7

EIGHT

8

NINE

9

www.ingramcontent.com/pod-product-compliance
Lightning Source LLC
Chambersburg PA
CBHW081003130726
48004CB00008BA/1843